DANCING WITH THE DEVILS

Memoirs of an Alcoholic, Drug Addicted Family

Brittney Owens

Dancing with the Devils
Copyright © 2022 by Melissa Sheridan

All rights reserved. No part of this publication may be reproduced, distributed, or transmitted in any form or by any means, including photocopying, recording, or other electronic or mechanical methods, without the prior written permission of the author, except in the case of brief quotations embodied in critical reviews and certain other non-commercial uses permitted by copyright law.

All Names have been changed to protect my family, friends and all involved.

ISBN
978-1-956529-54-8 (Paperback)
978-1-956529-53-1 (eBook)

This book is dedicated

In memory of my Loving Aunt

Table of Contents

Prologue vii
Chapter 1 Childhood 1
Chapter 2 Where it all began 11
Chapter 3 A dark family secret 23
Chapter 4 Getting help in therapy 37
Chapter 5 Al-Anon and Al-Ateen 49
Chapter 6 Getting help and hope for an Aunt 57
Chapter 7 My closest Aunt succumbs to Addiction 65
Chapter 8 My Sister's Addiction and Recovery 73
Chapter 9 My Sister's Rehab and After 93
Chapter 10 Change, Strength, Courage and Hope 109
Chapter 11 Serenity Prayer: Keep It Simple 117
Chapter 12 The Twelve Steps and Traditions 119
Epilogue 123
References 127

Prologue
◆ ◆ ◆

Here I am…… I never thought I'd see myself in one of these rooms. The room is quiet, you could hear a pin drop. It's small, chairs arranged in one complete circle. I see unfamiliar faces, some sullen, some hiding their face from shame and others sitting with newly found friends and support system. The brown paneled walls aren't too inviting. In all actuality it gives the room a somber, dreary feeling. Panic sets in as I take in all the emotions I feel from everyone and the room. I am shaking…. I am nervous….. I am scared…..

People pour into the door, I immediately tense up. Social settings make me panicky especially when I know no one. This is my first group. I don't think I have a problem, I shouldn't be here I scream in my head. The words race through my head over and over again, my palms become clammy and I begin to perspire as my chest races fast like a horse at the Kentucky derby. Everyone grabs a paper and clipboard and takes a seat in the circle of chairs. I glance over to see a young woman, there's an open seat next to her. She looks about my age, she looks very nice and who knew she was an addict being pregnant. I sit down next to her and introduce myself as does she. She proceeds to write on this paper labeled daily planner. I get up from my seat and grab a paper, pen and clipboard and return to my seat. I read the "daily planner" and wonder why? Why am I here? I have never done Heroine, coke, crack or any hard core drugs! I never touched any of that stuff not even pills! I just smoke marijuana; Alcohol is worse. Marijuana to me is Xanax it helps my panic and anxiety attacks. Not to mention it helps mask the emotions inside that stem from my childhood. So, yes I "self medicated" myself. What's the harm in that?

I look at the clock 10 after 10. This is going to be a *long* two hours. My body starts trembling as I look at the eight questions, panic sets in…. I don't belong here races through my mind. I don't have a problem; my problem was solved when I had my first joint 25 years ago.

A young woman, tall, skinny, with dirty blonde hair walks in. Everyone becomes silent as all eyes lay upon her. This must be our group leader Kathy and my new personal therapist for Drug Alcohol Therapy Services (DATS). She is tall, skinny, her pink lips smiles warmly at us. She seems very nice and personable. She introduces herself in a soft, warming voice and gives a little background on herself and how she became a drug and alcoholic therapist. "For those of you who are new, my name is Kathy. All of us would like to welcome you to our group. This is a non-judgmental zone, we're like Vegas here. What happens here stays here in this room. You can safely and comfortably know that you may speak your mind freely. Ok now that we've gotten the rules out of the way we'll start with our daily planners" My tension is put at ease. She speaks up "We'll start with our daily planners at this end of the room." All I can think of is Thank God I choose the right end of the room. I look at the questions and don't know what to write.

The room is filled with hardcore alcoholics and drug addicts whom were only there for drug court or because they were court mandated. The first gentleman starts to speak, "Hi, I'm G and I'm an alcoholic." The crowd speaks in harmony "Hi G, welcome." "I have been sober for 180 days." The room breaks out in cheers and whistles and signs of encouragement. I think to myself, ok maybe this isn't as bad as I thought, it seems like a positive group. He proceeds to tell the group his answers to the questions on his paper. Kathy looks at him and says, "G is there anything you'd like to share with group today?" G looks around the room; you can see tears start to swell in his eyes as he fights them back. He proceeds to tell us how he lost everything 180 days ago. How he'd been an alcoholic in denial for 25 years and his wife had had enough. He told us how his whole life went down the toilet. How he can only visit his children in a supervised social setting. Ever since then he has been battling to make things right and do what he needs to do to win his family back. A tear rolls down my cheek. My heart starts beating fast anticipating what the next person has to say. Is it worse? Is it not as bad? I don't think I can handle anymore. It feels like the room is shrinking as an overwhelming heat wave swarms me.

Everyone proceeds in the same routine. Hi I am so and so and I am a cocaine addict, hi I am so and so and I am a Heroin addict. I hear these people talk of being on drug court, colors and in and out of jail for selling and or doing drugs. Colors? What the hell are colors? I am screaming inside *I don't belong here*! I am not a criminal or forced here. I am here by my own choice realizing I had a major problem that I kept masked by my own addiction, hiding deep inside, burying it so far, so deep inside no one could get to my dark secret. One day it all just erupted like Mt. St. Helen. I called it self medicating myself. I never got in trouble like these people nor done any of these hard illicit drugs like them.

The next two people woke me up. They spoke positive about their addiction and their recovery. The positivity and strength in these people put me at ease and made me think. Now it's my turn. I pause… My face must've turned white because my group leader looked at me and said softly "It's ok, take your time. You don't need to share if you don't want to. We don't make you do things you don't want to do. You have a choice Brittney. If you'd like to share take a breath and when you're ready you may speak. Remember this is a non-judgmental zone and you can feel safe knowing what is said here stays here." I close my eyes and take a long breath… "Hi, my name is Brittney and I am an addict…

Chapter One:

Childhood

My mother and Father met in high school, they were like night and day, complete opposites in every way. My mom was the rich, could do no wrong teenager, while on the other side my dad was the typical I DON'T CARE, bad boy. He dropped out of school in the 10th grade. He was already into every kind of drug, was the life of the party. He was the coolest drug dealer in town. He sold things such as marijuana, cocaine, speed, LSD, acid, mescaline, etc… You name it he had it or if he didn't, he had that connection.

My parents worked at Channel; Channel was a department store similar to a K-Mart or Wal-Mart these days. Mom was the manger there while dad was a stock boy. Mom couldn't stand dad. He would always tease her and one day he stopped. They started hanging out with friends as friends. Then things grew from there.

My Parents dated for one and a half year before they decided to get married. On August 2nd, 1977 my parents were married. Just about one year and two months later I was born. My father didn't want children right away and didn't care much that they were having a baby. Mom told me this when I was older that he wasn't ready to grow up. My sister Kim arrived just 3 months shy of 2 years after I was born.

My mom had 1 full time job and a part time job, as my father had a full time job, a part time job and his side job just to make ends meet. Mom worked part time at a dinner then worked at a bar as a waitress at night after Dad came home. Dad worked as a mechanic for a gas station and worked part time for my mom's father in his construction business. They coordinated their schedules so they didn't need to pay for a babysitter. A lot of the time we spent with our great grandmother (mom's side) in Hopetown, NJ. She watched us and our Aunt Chelsea whom was only four years older than I.

My sister Kim wasn't your typical baby. She was a very colic baby and back then no one understood nor heard of what colic was. With mom's constant attention on Kim I was pushed aside, good thing I had an imagination and could keep myself entertained. When mom would come home from working two jobs at two am in the morning, she did everything to put Kim to sleep. Dad could never get Kim to stop crying he would always tell mom "She hates me. I just know it. She *hates* me!" Mom would show dad how to soothe her by bouncing her, rocking her, singing to her in a soft, soothing voice to the wee hours of the morning. Kim slept best in the swing as it move back and forth soothing her and finally putting her fast asleep. Mom would wake up and her busy day would start all over again... Dealing with all of this my mother was going through lymphphatic cancer. We couldn't afford chemotherapy for her so she volunteered for a government program to test a new cancer drug called Interferon. I watched my once beautiful mom become this worn out, feet dragging, slow moving with black bags under her eyes mother.

One day things changed with my mom. She began to have so much energy and moved so fast. I thought maybe dad finally gave her a break and took over for her and finally she got a good night's rest for once, instead of Dad going out to party all night or bringing the party home while I was in bed. It was 6 months of chemo on the interferon and mom's cancer was put into remission.

I started noticing things when I was three years old. I was woken out of a dead sleep to hear laughing and the voices of my dad, mom, Uncle Jim, Uncle Freddy and Uncle Dave. The others I did not know. I snuck out ever so quietly so I didn't wake Kim or let anyone know I was peeking around the corner. Halfway down, the hall was filled with smoke and this odor. To me as a three year old it smelt just like a skunk. Everyone was laughing and having a great time. They were reminiscing about childhood and the "good ole times." My 3 Uncle's have been my dad's best and closest friends since grade school, so they were family, like brothers. I watched as Uncle Jim passed what looked like a long cylinder thing with what looked like a bowl attached to it. He lit the bowl with his lighter and sucks the top then blew out all this smoke. He then passed it to Uncle Freddy. On the table I noticed a mound of pills and four straight lines of this white powder. I thought to myself, what was that? Is it baby powder? And those pills.... Were they baby aspirin? I was so confuse but still watched in astonishment. I was in awe as I watched my father roll up a twenty dollar bill and put into his nose and sniffed the baby powder! Ewe, gross, why? Then my mother went next! Now I had a disgusted face. I just didn't understand! My mom followed the baby powder up with 2 baby aspirins. I thought, oh now I know why she has so much energy now. Hmm who knew baby powder and aspirin. I shrugged my shoulders and went back to bed.

I was four years old and Kim was two when our little sister Krystal was born. It was now that my dad was ready to be a father. At this point I have become self-sufficient. Doing things for myself and trying to help mom out the best I could. What Kim couldn't do I did for her. Dad wouldn't change dirty diapers, so I was to change Krystal's diapers whenever mom wasn't around. Mom had become so energetic at this point in our lives. She'd work, come home to cook, get ready to go to job number two, cleaned up after dinner and get us ready for bed for dad all before she went into work. She pulled out a pill bottle and took two pills. I asked her what is that. She responded with a smile and a soft, loving voice and said "Sometimes when mommies work too hard and they get really bad headaches. These help them go away." She kissed us all and was off to work.

Mom came home around two in the morning that evening as Kim and I were woken out of a dead sleep by yelling. My dad and mom were arguing, you could tell by the tone of my dad's voice that he was very angry at mom. "*No more mescaline*! I will not get you anymore! You are getting way too addicted." We could hear my mom plead as she cried. I imagined her pleading at my father's feet, crying and begging like a dog. Dad stood his ground. Kim turned to me with pouty lips, eye brows scrunch as if she was lost and said "what's mesaline?" I said with anger on my face "those are mom's headache pills! Aw, poor mom. *I hate* dad!" My teeth were clenched, hands so tight fisted they were white, Kim noticed my expression and said " Yea me too!"

The next morning mom was sick. She called her boss at her job and told him she couldn't make it in today. She needed to take a sick day. That was unheard of, mom never, ever calls out of work. She even goes into work sick. Kim and I decided to get Krystal dressed and feed her breakfast for mom. After we took care of Krystal and put her in her swing, we decided to make mom oatmeal, being as that was the only thing I knew how to make. We put her food, napkin, spoon, oatmeal and coffee on a tray and I carried it into her bedroom. Her bedroom was dark, curtains closed, not one peep of sun shining through, it smelt of cigarette smoke and was kind of smoky as my eyes were burning, I turned on the light. Mom looked at us sleepy eyed, she smiled and said in a low, sincere tone "I love you girls! You're the best!" Kim and I looked at mom with a big smile turned to each other and smiled…. We were *proud* and felt special.

We moved to the Garden Apartments in Spring Ville, NY in 1983. The Garden Apartments were the worst choice my parents ever made. There were several brick buildings in a row two by two. It was what we would call "the projects" today. It was cheap rent for low income families. I remember very bad people and very few good people there. The playground was the worst. It had broken up asphalt that you had to be careful not to trip in or fall. The majority of the swings were crooked, there was one good swing besides the asphalt under them was so broken up it scared us. All around the ground of the playground was broken glass, trash, cigarette butts and needles.

My father started taking trips up to Pennsylvania; I can remember my dad telling mom how beautiful it was, how much cheaper and a wonderful place to raise their girls. He wanted to move us from the trash and the streets; he wanted something better for us than Spring Ville, NY. He started going up during the week looking for a place and a job. Before we knew it we were moving up to a town called Grand Rapids, Pennsylvania. He found us a 3 bed room, 1 bath house… *House*. Not an apartment building, an actual house with our very own back yard!

I was seven years old when we moved to Grand Rapids, PA. It was a secluded area, very woodsy. The smell of fresh pine and woods soothe my inner soul and made me feel at peace and safe. Grand Rapids was a little town where everyone knew everyone. It was the same faces you see day in and out. The town consisted of a very small little Grocery store, three bars, three churches and a Fire House. I thought to myself wow no wonder dad moved us up here, it's a gourmet feast of beer for him. I remember my mom cried for months to my grandmother saying "He moved us to the middle of nowhere!" Back in the 80's the area wasn't quite as big and commercialized as it is today. Every weekend we had to make a day trip to do our grocery and clothing/retail shopping at once. We had to travel 45 minutes away to either Montway, NY or to Scarlton, PA. Both directions were the same amount of time, but Scarlton was the safer area, we learned that fast.

We were settling in nicely. Mom got a night job at the Grand Rapids Casino which was the bar down the road from us. Dad worked for Medford Chrysler dealership as an auto technician during the day. I went to the Grand Rapids School House which was a four room school and across the church next to the Grand Rapids Casino. The top two rooms were 3rd and 4th grade and the bottom two rooms were 5th and 6th. Kim went to a three room school house in Lexington which was just south of Grand Rapids about half a mile. The school consisted of Kindergarten through 2nd grade. Next to the school was a church. Any parent who signed their child up for Religion class the 8th period of the day was what they called "Free time or religious education." The Nuns would come over to the school and line up all the children who were signed up and bring them over for class. This was back in the day when religion was still in schools.

By the time I was in 4th grade Western Valley Area School district had finished the North elementary school which consisted of Kindergarten through 4th grade; 5th-8th went to the middle school attached to the elementary school. The Religion kids were bused last period of the day to the church for class.

Mom and Dad adjusted nicely. They joined the Grand Rapids Volunteer Fire Department. Dad was a firefighter and had to go to fire school and mom joined the Ladies Auxiliary. It was there that mom met her very closest friends. After Krystal was in Kindergarten, Mom got a reception job at Medford Optical Center during the day and kept her evening job at the bar. She went from one job to the other.

After school, we'd come home and there would be a note for me. The note consisted of chores that needed to be done after our homework and what she took out for dinner to make before dad came home. I was nine years old and more like an adult rather than a child. At nine years old I had an alarm, woke myself up and then Kim; I was making Kim and my lunches for that day. She always complained that I put "too much" jelly on her peanut butter and jelly sandwich. Before we left for the bus I made sure to wake mom up to get ready for work. At eight years old I had too much responsibility; By the time I was ten I was like a young adult taking care of my sister's, the house and everything else needed to run a house hold. I had *no* childhood…

From the time mom got the job bartending at the Grand Rapids Casino; we spent ninety percent of the time there with our dad. Talk about boring… Dad would sometimes give us quarters to play some games; other friends of my parents also gave us some quarters to play games. That got old real quick and we're back to sitting at the table watching whatever the bar people wanted to watch. We basically grew up in the bar. Everyone then started bringing their kids to the bar. We would have our little "groupie" and play outside in the field behind the bar; nights wed play Ghost in the Graveyard.

The bar owners were husband and wife, the husband made the best pizza ever! Everyone ate The Grand Rapids Casino's Pizza. Sometimes when we were very bored, Carl the owner and pizza maker would invite us back and he would show us how the pizzas were made. Carl was tall about six foot two inches, he was a hefty guy with a beer belly. He had greasy black scraggly hair and brown eyes. He was always good with children, inventing new pizzas; like the chocolate chip pizza and the chocolate pretzel pizza. He would send mom home with one of his dessert pizza's just for us. He loved us....

I don't remember the exact age when it all began; maybe eight and a half or nine years old. I was always Carl's favorite; everyone even knew it, they weren't blind. Whenever he had us so called "Help" make the pizza, I always had to stand in front of him. I would have to roll out the dough; bending over as far as my little legs could reach and roll back down. At first it was the rubbing up and down slowly against my bum that made me uncomfortable. I could feel his pants stiffen. I would freeze and tense up, my heart beating fast; I didn't know what to do. My voice was shaky as I squeaked and handed over the rolling pin to Carl, "I don't know what else to do, here. I need to use the bathroom." I ran out of there.

I began to dread going into the kitchen as it still happened over and over, only now along with him rubbing behind me he has moved his hand in front of me and rubbing me where he shouldn't have been. I was so scared. I would tremble, my palms would sweat; the same words racing through my head over and over and over, *"Oh God, Please* make him stop, make him stop!" This point I hated going into the kitchen and refused to go in anymore until… One day my two sisters' begged me to go in. All that went through my mind was *Oh God if I am not there will he do what he did to me to my sisters?* So I went in slowly and cautiously. Carl had his head down rolling out the dough. My sisters' chanted together "Hi!" Carl looked up and smiled, he turned and saw me and his face lit up like a Christmas tree. He assigned Kim and Krystal their duties and they got to them right away.

Carl snickered at me "I've got a special job for you. I got a new machine." He grabs my waist and puts me in front of it and he positions behind me closely. He leans in close to me and moves my hair from my neck. I can feel his hot breathe against my neck and smelt the rotten smell of whiskey. "You take the dough with both hands, go on." I took the dough as his hands reach down to my hips and pulled them closer to him. I trembled and a tear ran down my face as I felt a huge bulge against me. He pulls me tighter and says "Now you thrust (as he thrusts his bulge deep towards my butt) the dough through both cylinders". My voice and hands shake as I say "Wow." Carl smiles "Now do the rest of them." I look on the table and see 15 more rolls of dough. I turn back so he can't see the tears escape my eyes. I am crying, I am screaming, I am dying inside... I slowly grab the next dough and Carl takes things a little further... I start shaking as he unbuttons my jeans; my heart is pounding out of my chest I am pleading to God right now for this nightmare to end! He slips his finger into my underwear and starts to rub as his other hand slinks up my shirt and plays with my chest. Inside I am screaming, I want to crawl out of my skin, *please someone, anyone come in here or call us!* He starts rubbing fast and then inserting his finger in and out. I start crying. I guess he could hear my sniffles because he stopped. "Ok girls that's enough helping for today. Thank you."

Carl stared taking us to church on Sunday's as a favor to our parents. They weren't too much of practicing Catholics but we needed to get our Sacraments. Carl would pick us up early and take us to breakfast then to church and class. After class he would take us to the old country store across the PA/NY Bridge. We were always excited to go there as we knew it very well from years of going summer after summer camping at Roaring Rapids Camp grounds.

Carl smiled as our faces lit up; walking down each isle trying to decide what snack we wanted. "You girls can have whatever you want. Pick a couple of things." We were over excited and proceeded to pick several items of cookies and candies. Kim and Krystal decided to indulge themselves in there snacks when we get into the car, I noticed as I glance back through the rearview mirror. Carl noticed too and looked at me with a sneer. "Do you want to drive?" I got excited as a ten year old not knowing my fate. "YES!" I exclaimed excitedly. "Slide over a little more and grab the wheel." I did as asked, I was nervous. I had never taken the wheel before and drove the car in between the two lines. It was a lot harder than I thought. Then I realized my palms started sweating as his hands made way to my shorts and pushed my thighs apart; starting to rub between the warmth of my thighs. I froze and panicked, swerving the car to distract him. My plan worked as he stopped and grabbed the wheel to regain control. "I'm sorry Carl; guess I'm just not ready yet."

This went on for two months. I told no one, I felt disgusted in myself. I began dreading going to church and pleaded with mom to take us. In church I prayed hard for this nightmare to end. I prayed and prayed; day and night and still my nightmare continued. I began to lose all hope in God and began to become a nonbeliever. *Why would he allow this to happen to me? Why would he think I deserve this?* It was a year before my Confirmation that my nightmare finally ended. My mom finally started bringing us to church regularly.

With mom working all the time and dad working and spending bill money on his alcohol problem I was the caretaker of my two younger sisters. I had become mother hen to them. They looked to me for help with school work and looked up to me as if I were mom. I had always had that motherly instinct; Mom and family always said I had the patience of a Saint when it came to children and babies. We came home from school: It was the same old routine, homework, chores, and then I made what mom took out for dinner that night. I made sure my sisters both got showers and laid their clothes out for school the next day. I went from a seven year old to a young lady, then a thirteen year old to an adult. When I say I had no childhood, I really had no childhood! I learned responsibility at a very young age; it was forced upon me due to my irresponsible, Alcoholic father.

Chapter Two:

Where it all began

I was thirteen years old when I was able to get working papers from Wallenpaupack School. Back then there were no Cinderella hours, or limited hours for minors. My father got me a job at O'Malley's Pub in Stanton, PA. It was a very busy bar and restaurant. I was hired as a bus person for four nights a week and got paid $15.00 a shift and 10% of the waiter/waitresses' tips. For me it was good pay. The dining room had 30 tables and at times it would turn over two times a night and on weekends three times a night; I was the only bus person. Some nights I wouldn't get out of there until 2-3 in the morning and still had to wake my sisters and myself up for school the next day.

 Dad told me if I wanted to drive when I was sixteen I had to save my money to buy a car and pay my own insurance. Well that never happened. One morning I hear Mom crying at the kitchen table. She and dad fought the night before and he walked out slamming the door behind him and peeling out of the driveway. I know because I was woken up from all the arguing and screaming. I checked on my sisters across from my room; they were both in Kim's bed holding each other underneath the blankets. I hoped into bed with them and put my arms around them to console them. I start to sing to them to calm and soothe my sisters.

Before I woke Kim and Krystal up I sat down at the table and asked mom why she was crying. Wiping tears away from her red, swollen eyes she said softly "Don't worry Britt; mommy and daddy are just a little behind on our bills. But we will manage." She smiled at me. I got up from the table and went to my room. I was angry; angry at my dad for drinking their money away! Under my bed I kept a jewelry box with a lock on it, it had my most precious jewelry in it and all the money I had made so far from O'Malley's. So far I had saved up $856.00. I grabbed the money and sat back down at the table; I watched mom as she flipped through the pile of bills. "Mom, I want to help, and I don't want to hear no from you." I passed the wad of cash across the table to her. "It's what I have been saving so far and I want you to have it to help pay the bills." Mom's mouth dropped as she counted it. "Britt, I appreciate this but I can't take this. You shouldn't have to worry about adult stuff." I looked at her eyes wide open, "And you shouldn't have to work two jobs to support dad's drinking, just to make bills we can't make." "I insist you take my money, its mine and I choose what I want to do with it!!" Mom looks at me proudly, "How did I get so lucky to have such a wonderful, amazing daughter as you?" I smiled proudly and hugged her.

I had worked at O'Malley's Pub for six months, when it all began. The staffers were all men except for one woman who was the bartender and the owner's daughter. My parents always said that I had a magnetic personality; that everyone always flocked to me and liked me from the start. I was naive to begin with and had been taken advantage of and mistaken niceness and friendliness for what men took as me flirting with them. The Kitchen staff were all men; Joe was the owner and cook, Tom was his prep and back up chef, Pete the waiter, Peggy the waitress and Matt was the dishwasher.

Matt was nineteen years old, tall, skinny; he had brown hair and gorgeous blue eyes. I have to say I did have a bit of a crush on him, what girl wouldn't? He always smiled at me as I came into the kitchen to drop off dirty dishes. I couldn't help to notice his nice butt as he was bent over the sink scrubbing a pan. I shook the thought off and concentrated on my work. Thinking to myself, table 28 needs four salad plates. I go to the back room and go into the walk in refrigerator to get the salads. The door opens, Tom comes in. I wonder why he's in here… Tom was in his early thirties, he had short, curly, brown hair and green eyes. He wasn't very much taller than I was, maybe about 5"8' tall. He was a good looking guy and quite the jokester.

Tom slowly inches closer to me, "I've been noticing you lately."

My voice squeaks as my heart pounds, "Oh yea. Well I have to go; I have to bring these to the table. We're very busy out there. Bye." I rush around him and struggled to open the door with four salad plates in my hands. I feel Tom put his hand gently on my butt and gently squeeze as finally the door opens and I escape to the dining room.

It's one in the morning I cleared the last of the tables and gathered all the linens together. Pete was the waiter on duty for the night: he is counting his tips. Pete had short blonde hair and crystal blue eyes. The most beautiful blue eyes I had ever seen; they were like looking down in the clearest blue sea. He was a short and stocky young man and somewhat attractive. He was quite the flirtatious fellow flirting with every woman that came into the bar and restaurant; not to mention the staff as well.

I bring the last of the dishes into the kitchen; Matt and Tom are breaking things down and cleaning up. I have to bring the linens upstairs to the washroom and start them in the washer and the owners switch them to the dryer when they close up. I hated going to the washroom the hallway was dark with a dim light and the washroom was at the end of the hallway. That room too had a dim light; the place was old and had an eerie feeling about it. As I load the wash I feel as if someone is watching me; a chill runs up my spine. My heart races out of my chest as I feel hot air sweep across my neck; the hair raising on my arms.

"Here are your tips for tonight." Pete whispers softly in my ear, slipping the money slowly in the front pocket of my apron.

Holding my breath I breathe out, "Oh Pete, You scared me. Thank you very much. I'm done here. Have a great night. Dad's waiting for me, Bye." I quickly ran down the stairs.

Months passed and I endured flirting, groping and other stuff that was shameful from all three men. I kept thinking back to washing the linins and Pete always coming up and fondling me and pushing my head down towards his groin shoving my face into his exposed manhood pushing my head up and down. This happened every night I worked with him. I *hated* going to the wash room. I kept thinking to myself, *why me? Why? Is this my fault? Did I somehow give them the wrong impression and they thought my kindness was flirtatious?* Although I felt disgusting and shameful in myself; I kind of felt beautiful and special that three men were interested in me. I thought to myself, *is that so wrong? Maybe this is my entire fault! Yes, I must've led them on…..*

A year later Matt and his girlfriend Abby were looking for an apartment. Their landlord wasn't fixing anything that broke in their place and got fed up. It just so happen that one evening, Matt and my father were talking. I tried to listen in at the conversation as I got a table their sodas from the bar. But heard nothing. Later on that evening I was smoking a cigarette outside; which I started smoking when I was ten. I was now fourteen and had been working at O'Malley's for almost two years. I sat down in the chair, how wonderful it felt to finally have a break after turning the dining room over three times that Saturday evening. It didn't help that we had live music and the atmosphere was happy and in good company with friends and families. Matt came out to smoke. My heart fluttered; even though he had a girlfriend I still thought he was gorgeous and still had a crush on him. We started chatting, friendly talk about this and that. He started leaning in towards me, my heart was pounding, palms sweaty and my breath quickened. I thought; what's he doing? Is he going to kiss me? Nah, he has a girlfriend. I can feel the warmth of his breath on my neck as the hairs on my arm rise as I get goose bumps. I had never had felt this before. He speaks softly in my ear, my body trembles. He knows as he smiles looking into my eyes, "Guess what?"

My voice starts to squeak and I clear my voice as I compose myself. "What?"

"I was telling your dad about how I was looking for a place to rent. He said that he had just had someone move out of your parent's apartment downstairs and was looking for someone to rent it." His face had the biggest smile I've ever seen.

I take a deep breath, "That's great. When do you and Abby move in?"

"In two weeks, I can't wait!" He seemed so excited, I didn't know how to feel. I guess I had mixed feelings.

It was the same old routine at O'Malley's, Tom and Pete continued doing what they did. I felt disgusting and went home each night and *scrubbed* my body as if it had be tainted. As if I washed all the sin away. Matt started to change a few weeks after he moved in downstairs; men talking and bragging to each other. We had a commercial freezer in the downstairs hallway across from the storage room and right next to the apartment door. Mom always asked me to go down and take something out for diner that evening as Kim and Krystal were "too scared" to go downstairs. I roll my eyes at my sisters and obey mom's instructions. The first time I went down,

Matt came out when he heard rummaging outside the door; he noticed the noise and opened the door to see me.

"Hi." He smiled. "I've been wondering when I'd be able to get you alone."

Huh, I thought to myself. Ok now I am wigged out. "Brittney, can I kiss you?"

"What?" I was confused, he noticed. "But what about...." Before I could finish my sentence he had leant in and started to kiss me. I had never been kissed before. He parted my lips and stuck his tongue in my mouth as his hands held my face gently. My heart raced, body quivered, I felt as if I were going to explode. All I thought was wow. Then I thought *this is wrong, it's not right*. The words raced through my head.

Months passed I continued to get groped and molested, things with Matt progressed a bit further and I was becoming very uncomfortable with his advances especially when he'd take me into the storage room and unzipped his pants and forced me to perform sexual acts on him. I was embarrassed, it was completely my fault. I led him on; he must've noticed that I had a crush on him. I kept this dark secret to myself pushing it deep down inside just as I did with what I endured with Carl. No one knew, not a single person; not even my best friend and sister Kim. I told her everything. But all that has happened to me I felt ashamed would she judge me, would anyone else judge me??

Every time I had to go down to the freezer I begged and pleaded with Mom and of course I never won. I always tried to sneak in and be so quiet so Matt didn't hear me; but it never worked. He must've seen me walk by his kitchen window; it was always the thing every time. Afterwards he'd go into the apartment and I would slide down the wall and cry softly. I wiped my tears away and composed myself, got dinner out and went upstairs.

I started skipping school with a group of my friends; it consisted of seven of my closest, dearest friends; we were a group not to be messed with. We stuck up for each other and if one was in a fight we'd all pounce on the prey like a pack of wolves. No one messed with us, they knew better! We would eat lunch and after sneak out of the school and go across the street to Henry's convenient store. Next to the store was an old abandoned building that we would go and "hang out" in. We were fourteen years old, barely driving. We thought we were cool, smoking cigarettes and smoking our first joint. I remember it like it was yesterday, the taste of it. The smell and the way it made me feel. I felt giddy, all my troubles were gone; it put me at ease…..

I was a light smoker in the beginning; only smoking with my friends when we skipped class. I never went to work or school stoned, I was a closet smoker. I wasn't sure if people would be able to tell if I was high or if they could smell it on my clothing.

It was the same night at work. I was exhausted it was a very busy evening and I didn't even have time to get a break or eat dinner. I collected all the linens walked slowly towards the hallway and laid them down on the stairs. I peeked into the kitchen, I heard all three men talking and laughing. I thought to myself thank goodness. I quickly ran up the stairs, threw the linens in and started them. I ran down the stairs and to the bar I went where my dad would be waiting for me. My heart skipped a beat, where was he? I ran out the front door, his car was not there. I go to the waiter/waitress station and pick up the phone. Pete comes out of the kitchen.

"Oh, Brittney your dad asked me to bring you home tonight."

My heart race and my voice was shaky "Oh, he did. He didn't tell me."

"Here are your tips. Are you ready to go?" It almost seemed like he was excited. My tone was low "Yea."

"Ok. I just need to get my car keys from my house, follow me." Panic set it, I was scared…. My stomach started to turn and I could feel the vomit come half way up my throat.

Pete's house was only fifteen feet from O'Malley's. We got there and he went up the stairs as I stood at the bottom of the stairs. "Come on in Britt ." He said with a grin.

"I think I'll wait for you out here." Pete comes down by me and goes behind me. He gently puts his hands on my back and pushes me up the stairs. "Don't be silly. It's the middle of winter, you'll freeze to death." I push the door open; there was a manly, eerie smell about the place. It seemed to be the typical bachelor pad.

"I just have to get my keys from the bedroom." He waves me on as he walks down the hallway. I freeze… "I'll just stay here." I see the light on down the hallway, it flickers then goes off. Pete sounding annoyed says "Damn fuse! *Ow*!"

I hear a loud thud. "Pete? I pause. Pete? Are you ok?" I feel a hand from below grasp my leg and I let this blood curling scream out.

"It's ok Britt. It's just me. I hit my shin on the corner of my bed and fell."

I breathe a sigh of relief. "Can I have some help up please?" I help Pete to his feet; he pulls me close to him and hugs me. "Thank you so much." He whispers in my ear sending a shiver down my spine.

I hesitate, pushing him away, but he is stronger than me and resists. "Pete, you're hurting me."

"I'll make you feel better." He throws me backwards on the bed getting on top of me. Pinning me down by my wrists, his body on top of me; he starts licking my ear and slowly moves down my neck up towards my mouth.

"You starting to feel better?" Scared I stumble over my words "No, pppleasse stooo..." Before I could finish he thrusted his tongue in my mouth and engulfed my mouth and tongue. His free hand slided up my shirt and under my bra. He pinched my nipple and I screamed, my voice muffled by his tongue in my mouth. His hand moves down and unbuttons my pants, then unzips them, wiggling them off exposing my underwear. I think to myself *Oh God please NO, stop him!* "Pete, please stop! I don't want to do this!" His head goes under my shirt and starts licking and sucking on my breast. Tears stream down my face, "No stop please, Pete." He still ignores my plea as his hand slips down into my underwear and starts rubbing.

Help I scream in my head! My tears are now flowing like a river, doesn't he notice? As his hand continues to rub I feel a finger rub around my genitals as it penetrates deep within. With his finger going in and out over and over again; I try to wiggle free, but he is just too strong and heavy. "*Stop now*! You're hurting me Pete, please! I beg you stop!" He takes his hand out of my underwear and I feel relieved.

Pete grabs what looks like two towels; he pulls me up by my wrists to the top of the bed. What is he doing? He begins to tie one hand tight to one bed post and does the same to the other. I freak out, struggling to break free, kicking my feet at him. "Feisty aren't we. So you like it rough. So do I." He sounded more sinister now. I am shaking, scared to death now. There is no use screaming, no one is around, no one can help me now. I cry. Pete licks around my nipples and slides his tongue down my belly as his hands pull my under wear down. He unbuttons his pants siding them down along with my underwear. I try one more desperate plea. "Pete, please. I don't want to do this, you're hurting me can't you see? *Please* I am scared." He snickers "Everyone is afraid the first time. Plus I know this is what you want, you're denying it. I've seen the way you look at me, undressing me and looking at the bulge in my pants. Oh God

Brittney you turn me on!" He points to his manhood which is hard and huge by now. "See what you do. Now it's my turn to make you feel the same way. Enjoy." I cry pleading *"No* Pete, I never gave you any idea this is what I wanted. Please don't do this! I'm begging you." He looks up at me and smiles as if we were in love and we were making love together. I was disgusted, I was crying....

He parts my legs and gets down on his knees putting his face into my genitals. He starts licking in circles, he glances up at me seeing me cry. "Oh, don't cry baby, I just need to get you wet and I promise you it won't hurt at all." He speaks softly and proceeds doing what he started. He starts flicking his tongue up and down along my genitals, then side by side. My tears are now flowing like Niagara and my cry turns to a wail. His tongue began to thrust inside me in and out in and out. *"No, No, No!* Stop Pete!!!" He thrusts his manhood deep inside my vagina; my eyes bulge out as it seems as though my heart stops and I freeze. I scream out loud as Pete smiles thrusting in and out over and over again. I see a look of satisfaction smeared all over his face as he moans and grabs me close. I cry and then screamed at him "It hurts! I told you to stop!" Pete looks at me disgusted and angrily as his tone confirms this "Get up. Time to go!" He throws my clothes at me and unties my wrists.

When I get home I unlock the door and quietly enter the house as it is two thirty in the morning. I go into the bathroom and start the shower. I am crying as I undress throwing my clothing in a pile by the corner. I go to the bathroom and wipe. I cry there is blood on the toilet paper. I get into the shower, scrub my body; I scrub so hard that my body is red. I slide down the shower and sit in the bath tub knees up to my chest and head down. I am still crying; though the beating hot water seems to be soothing. I noticed in the mirror when I walked into the bathroom, my eyes were swollen, red and puffy.

"Britt?" A very sleepy Kim walks into the bathroom, closing the door quietly behind her. "Britt, are you Ok?" I sniff, wipe my face and try to compose myself. "I am ok Kim, no worries." Kim rips the shower curtain wide open. *"BS!"* She looked at me, her eyes seeing right through me. Kim is my best friend, she knows me inside out. I turn the shower off and grab my towel wrapping it around me. I look her in the eyes seriously "You got to promise me something. What I am about to tell you, no matter how *good* or how *bad* you cannot tell a single person. You must take this to your grave!" I grab her shoulders my eyes meeting hers as a tear runs down my face. "Britt, you're scaring me. I promise you know me." I turn around I can't face her, I feel so disgusting… So ashamed… I feel like a slut… I am crying now, Kim grabs me and hugs me. She rubs my back reassuring me that she is the only person I can tell my darkest secrets to. I sniffle "I was raped by Pete tonight." There is silence… Kim starts crying and pulls me close and holds me tight. "Oh Britt, I am so sorry! We will get through this. I promise." Kim took my clothing, held my hand and threw the clothes in the garbage. "See forgotten." I smile, "Thanks"

A couple of weeks go by, Pete doesn't talk to me. In fact he doesn't even acknowledge me, except to give me my tips. I liked it that way; no more laundry room incidents. I was relieved. After the Pete incident I had increased my smoking of marijuana. I was smoking every day a couple times a day. Well the *majority* of the day and it was beginning to become very costly. I didn't care, it helped me control my emotions, and it made me forget. Forget that horrible night. That night that haunts me over and over each time I close my eyes. I had become an Insomniac.

I started to grow marijuana to offset my costs. Growing marijuana under my parents' nose was a very easy task. My mom was oblivious to everything, she was so naive and dad was barely home. I grew it right in my own bedroom closet and no one even knew or ever found out about it. I had so much I didn't even need to buy it anymore. My addiction became worse as time went on.

I had been working at O'Malley's for two years now only three weeks before was that dreadful night. Pete had quit and moved for a better job in Newtown, NJ. I was so glad that I didn't have a constant reminder of that dreadful night. Abby and I had become very good friends which Matt didn't quit like at all. It was a Saturday; Matt came up to talk to my father who was in the computer room as usual on a weekend day. Matt comes walking down the hallway smiling. "Hey Britt, your father said you can come to Wal-Mart with me and help me pick out a birthday gift for Abby." I look at him, hmmm. "I know you guys have gotten close and I am a man,

I don't know the first thing about women and what they want." I look at him, "Ok." I go to grab my jacket and say bye to my father.

We're driving home from Wal-Mart after getting Abby's gift; things seem very quiet and odd. I try to start conversation. "So Abby's birthday is tomorrow? Right?" Matt's eyes stay on the road, "Yea, and thanks for helping me." "You're Welcome." I notice he pulls down a dirt road. My heart races. "Uh, is this a short cut? I think you made a wrong turn." Matt turns to me and smiles softly, "Yea it's a short cut." I feel a bit relieved until he pulls over into high brush. "Matt, why did you stop?" He opens the door and says "Excuse me I have to go really bad and can't hold it." He closes the door. Time passes; I think to myself *gee why is he taking so long?* The door opens and I see a half naked Matt, he is naked from the waist down. I see his manhood and it is huge and bulging. I think *Oh God No!* "*Matt not you, please don't do this. I don't want to. Please....*" He pulls my legs down the seat as I kick and scream no. He laughs as if this is some game to him. He tears my pants and underwear off and I turn on my knees and crawl to my door trying to open it to escape. He grabs my hips and hold them tightly, rubbing his harden manhood against my vagina. "Matt please no. Don't do this!" He grins then snickers at me "I hear you like it rough. Well whore I will give it to you rough! Are you ready slut?" "Nooooo, *No!*" With those words he thrust his huge manhood deep into my vagina. My whole face slams against the window with the force of a hurricane. I feel a tear as I let out a blood curling scream. He continues to thrust in and out hard and fast as my face hits the widow with each thrust; I cry. He reaches up my shirt and pulls my bra up and squeezes my breast hard, then my nipples he pinches and rolls hard between his fingers as he thrusts deeper and deeper.

"You like it like this, don't you?" Tears roll down my face, my wailing stopped. I feel nothing, I am numb.........

I quit O'Malley's that week. I couldn't stay there any longer. I didn't want to have a constant reminder; plus he thinks I'm a slut and whore. Now everyone will know guys really do talk. Who would be next? Oh God, Tom. I just could handle any more traumatic experiences. Matt and Abby moved out a month later. I was so relieved; I never saw or heard from him again.

Chapter Three:
A dark family secret

1994-1995

I started my sophomore year in high school and Kim was finally a freshman. We were always best friends; though I always had to show her who was boss and the Alpha. She respected me and looked up to me. We hung out with the same crowd of friends; friends from all different cliques and grades. We were always there for each other, no one messed with us. She was the brains and I was the brawns. My whole attitude changed when I turned sixteen; I became very dominate, no one would ever hurt me, *ever* again! I began looking for submissive, non-dominate men for boyfriends as I would have the upper hand and nothing and no one could hurt or control me ever again. I knew this was a sickness of mine. But this was the only defense mechanism I had to protect myself from anyone trying to ever harm me again.

It was the beginning of November, three days before my cousin Randy was getting christened. My mom was Godmother and decided to go down Thursday evening to help my Aunt prepare. My father would come down Friday after we got out of school. Friday morning flew by, and it was time for my favorite subject Anatomy & Physiology. The phone rings, the teacher talks then hangs up.

"Brittney, you are to report to the office with all your things to go home."

"Ok." I grab my books and put them in my back pack and walk out the door. I'm confused. I didn't know dad was picking us up early. I shrugged off my confusion. I walk into the office; there is a somber feeling in the room. It gives me chills. One of the secretaries directs me down the hall to the guidance office. In passing I notice Kim in a room crying, her eyes red and puffy. I mouth, "You ok, what's wrong?" She shakes her head. I walk into the guidance office to see the principle, my guidance counselor, the school psychiatrist, a man I had never seen before and a police officer. *Oh God*, what is going on I think.

"Sit down Brittney. We need to talk to you and ask you questions." There is a man I do not know; I look at him disgusted and glare at him "And who are you?" "Brittney, I am your Lawyer, Mr. Miller and also Carson County's DA." I look at him confused "My lawyer?" My guidance counselor speaks up "Brittney I want you to know that Miss Davis and I are here for you. Corporal Anderson has to talk to you." I look to the police officer, thinking the worst. Thinking maybe dad got into an accident because he was too drunk and died.

"Miss Owens, may I can you Brittney or Britt? He seemed sincere, but I wasn't. In a sassy tone I said "It's a free country." I could see the embarrassment on everyone's face. I didn't care. Corporal Anderson hesitated "Ok, Ms. Brittney. I am here today because it has been brought to my attention that you may have been molested." My mouth dropped, I was furious *"Absolutely* not!" I think to myself, how could she, she said she would keep my secret I've kept hidden for two years. That's why she was crying, she knew she had broken her promise to me, she was ashamed.

"Well Miss Owens, both your sisters' have told their guidance counselors that your father has been molesting all of you for several years now." I stare at him silently; I don't know what to say. Is this some kind of sick joke? Why haven't my sisters mentioned any of this to me? After all I'm the one who's been there for them all our lives.

"No! No that's Bull Shit. They're lying! My dad never laid a finger on me or them. They have never told me anything and they always tell me everything!" I look at the cop angrily; if looks could kill he'd be dead.

Corporal Anderson's tone changes, it is more stern "Miss Owens, I don't think you understand. We have two confessions that they have both been molested by your father as early as last night. They both also said it has been happening to you as well, they have witnessed it on occasions. Now I want you to tell me the truth." I look at everyone in the room through squinted eyes as if to intimidate them. The last person I look at is Corporal Anderson; I fold my arms and look at the clock.

For five minutes the room is silent, Miss Davis clears her throat. "Well Brittney, would you like to talk to me, maybe privately?" She looks at me in a motherly way, her voice so soft and sincere. I smile, and then my face shows no expression. I look to the cop and speak low and angrily "Where are my sisters? I want to see my sisters'? I need to make sure there ok." He looks at me and speaks "Well I am sorry Miss Owens, but that is not possible. But know that they are ok."

I scream "Where ARE my sisters? They need me, they must be scared!" "Miss Owens you must calm down, please. Your sisters' are fine, they went home with friends. Your mom has been notified and is on her way up. I am sorry to say but when your father gets home he will be arrested." I start to cry. Miss Davis walks over and rubs my back trying to console me. I push her away. "Can I go home now?" "No you can't your coming with me Miss Owens." Corporal Anderson led me out of the office and out the door.

We arrive at the State police building. Corporal Anderson opens the back door and lets me out. "Why am I here? Why am I at the state police station; Am I being arrested?" I begin to panic and feel an attack set in; my chest feels like it's going to collapse. The police car seems to get smaller and smaller.... The air is slowly dissipating. Nothing .... He doesn't answer; he doesn't look back at me. We go in and he prompts me to sit down on the bench. He goes over to this elder woman; she has short grey hair and looks over worked and tired. They start talking. I hear them whispering, hearing few word such as uncooperative, disobedient, Mrs. White and foster parent. After talking, the woman sifts through a black book of phone numbers and starts dialing a number. Corporal Anderson grabs my arm and leads me to a room and shuts the door.

"Sit down Miss Owens." I glare at him and fold my arms "Thanks but no. I'm fine standing. Plus I don't take orders from strangers." "Really, so where do you get your attitude from your dad?" Now he really pissed me off. "Life lessons and jackasses like you!" He stands, up his chair flying across the room and hitting the wall. "You're pushing me Miss Owens'. One more sass mouth from you and I'll send you to a Juvenile detention home." I look at him, a tear streams down my face as I try to stay composed and so adult like. He then interrogates me like I'm some kind of criminal. Why? Why, am I being treated like this? Because I told the truth, that my father never laid a hand on me and I have never seen him do the same to my sisters'. The interrogation continues for about twenty minutes, same questions over again and again. Still my answers the same. Corporal Anderson walks out of the room, the look of frustration on his face. I am concerned now. It is six o'clock pm and I have not heard anything about my sisters' or mom. Plus I needed to call Abby to let my dogs out and feed them. I clear my throat, "Excuse me! *Excuse me*!" A woman's voice comes over the speaker, "Yes Miss Owens, what would you like?" Her voice is pleasant and warming; I couldn't be mean to her. "Yes mam, please I'd like to know how my sisters' are doing, I am worried about them. I also need to call my parents tenants to let my dogs out and feed them." "I'm sorry Miss Owens, but I was told no phone calls."

Thirty minutes pass by as I stare at the clock; panic sets in. Why am I here? I am being treated worse than a criminal. All of a sudden I hear muffled talking outside my door, mom? I think yay mom is here; I let out a sigh of relief. The door opens slowly, in walks in a middle aged woman. She looks to be in her mid forties, tall with salt and pepper colored hair. She smiles softly as she looks at me. "Hi Brittney, my name is Mrs. White but you may call me Brenda. Do you have any nicknames? I would like you to feel as comfortable and welcomed as you can for the duration of your stay." In a quiet, whimpering voice, I try to hide my sadness as I speak, "its Britt, everyone calls me Britt." "Will it be ok for me to call you Britt?" My face down, I nod. "I am here to bring you to stay with me until your mother picks you up. I am sure you would like my other foster children, I have about two girls that are your age." Foster home? I look at her then at Corporal Anderson "Why am I going to a foster home? Cant I just go with a friend like my sisters' have?" Mrs. White speaks in a low soothing tone as she places her hand on my shoulder, "I'm sorry Britt but no, you need to come with me." Panic sets in, the adrenaline pumps through my veins and I cry. "It's ok Brittney you're in good hands." She hugs me tight, reassuring me that she is sympathetic, not like the cop.

Its pitch black outside, except for the few lights in the parking lot of the state police building. It's typical for roads to be dark and unlit in Cornet County; we don't have any street lights. We travel down the darkened road for about thirty minutes making a right down a dirt road which led to a driveway. The house was inviting. It was three stories tall, white with pale blue trim and a white picket fence. We go through the locked gate; the yard had a playground area in one corner; the other was a patio with a grill, two picnic tables and chairs. Mrs. White opens the door; there is an aroma of pot roast cooking. I know this because I have made it a many times for dinner. My mouth waters as I have not eaten since breakfast. It's been a long day, I'm exhausted, hungry and want to go to bed and just cry myself to sleep. I hear banging and children laughing and screaming. Six kids of all ages from four to 17 years of age run around the corner and freeze, staring right at me as if they were looking through me like a glass mug. Mrs. White introduces us to each other and the kids make me feel welcomed. They were polite, well mannered and disciplined. Mrs. White served diner to us all and we said Grace before we ate.

After diner the kids all get up and each one proceeds to do his or her chore; either it be doing dishes, clearing the table, putting food away, etc... I turned to Mrs. White and asked her if I may speak to her in private. She led me into the living room and gestured for me to sit by her.

"Mrs. White...."

"Please Brittney call me Brenda."

"Ok, Brenda. Has my father been arrested?" My voice shaky.

"Yes he has been, earlier this evening. I'm sorry Britt" She holds my hand gently as a tear rolls down my cheek.

"When will my mother be coming to get me?"

"I'm afraid not tonight. The social worker couldn't get a hold of her.

But I promise I will try hard to keep calling until I get her. But until we do you have to stay here." She says with a smile. It was reassuring.

"Ok, Brenda I need to call my parents tenants who live downstairs to have them let my 3 dogs out and feed and give them water."

"I am sorry Brittney, but you are not allowed to call anyone. It's the rules and I would let you if I could but I cannot break the rules."

I start sobbing. She grabs me and holds me tight for a moment then gets up and walks into the kitchen. All I could think of was how scared my sisters' must be and my poor dogs have been locked up all day with no food and water and going outside to go to the bathroom. Mrs. White goes into the kitchen and instructs the kids to go do their daily bedtime routine. Shower schedules were posted outside each of the three bathrooms. My name was on the third floor as was my room. My shower time was at eight-thirty pm. I took my shower; clothes were already laid out for me in my bedroom. I change and sat down with the rest of the crew. They were watching TV and all I wanted to do was cry; they didn't even know I was dying inside. I excused myself and said goodnight. That night I cried myself to sleep.

I woke up the next morning hopeful. Mom should be getting me today, I just know it, she wouldn't leave me in this home like this. I quickly get out of bed and run down the stairs; I am the first one up. I see Brenda in the kitchen, she shoos me up the stairs, "we never come downstairs in our nightwear." I turn around and roll my eyes and run to my bedroom. Three minutes later I am downstairs and back in the kitchen.

"When is my mom coming to get me today?" I said excitedly.

"Britt I've been trying all morning, I can't get a hold of the social worker or your mom." My face changes from excitement to disappointment. I excuse myself and run to my room. I bury my face into my pillow and scream then cry. I stay here all day waiting to hear some good news. Brenda comes up several times to give me updates and try to get me to come down to eat but I don't respond. She pouts and leaves me be.

Saturday went by slow as I anxiously wait and wait for mom to come get me. But still no word from her. Why? What about my sisters'? Did she get them? What if no one is telling her where I am? What if their trying to keep me here to try and get me to lie!!! I scream loud, scaring the younger children. Brenda runs in looking all frazzled and worried, "What? What happened Brittney?"

"Nothing. Where's my mom!?"

"Hun, I found out that you have to stay here until Monday. The social worker's office is closed on weekends."

I grit my teeth, "Please leave me!"

Brenda gets up slowly, "I am here if you need me." She turns slowly walking out the door and shuts it quietly.

Saturday and Sunday went slower than a snail. A lot was rattling through my brain. I was going through withdrawal from not smoking, it helps calm me, keeps me from panicking and keep me in control of my situations. I was worried about my sisters' and now my mom, worried if I was stuck here and going to be one of those kids stuck in the system. My breathing quickened, I couldn't breathe. I could feel pain in my chest as I was gasping for air. I started kicking my feet on the bedroom floor to get someone's attention to help. I felt faint as I tried to catch my breath. Oh God I'm going to die. Brenda runs up the stairs like a bat out of hell and into my room. She automatically goes right into action keeping calm, cool and collect. Holding me with my back against her chest, she instructs me to follow the movement of her chest and breath in slowly and out slowly. Within minutes I was breathing normal and calmed down.

"Britt, I heard from the social worker today. She got a hold of your mom and she is on her way." I turned around and squeezed Brenda tight as tears rolled down my cheeks. Only these tears were of joy and happiness. My mom was finally coming to get me.

Being in the state barracks, interrogation room and a foster home was very traumatic for me. I was a child, barely 16 and was treated like a criminal. Mom was furious about the whole ordeal. We were all home at last except for dad. Grandma posted bail but the judge ordered him not to be anywhere around us until his trial is finalized and if guilty, sentencing is set. Mom had made an appointment with our lawyer who was the Cornet county DA. He was arrogant, short, and chubby and had grey hair. Us girls being of Italian decent can't help to allow our Italian temper show; we just react without thinking. A lot of times we embarrass mom. He starts by talking to us one by one, asking question after question. He asked very personal questions, myself and Krystal glared at him with our arms folded giving him the evil eye. I speak up, "I don't think any of this is your business *S I R*!" "Brittney Ann!" My mom was appalled. Krystal then opens her mouth. She is our sassy, spiteful little sis, who isn't afraid to say what she thinks. "My father never touched us. Besides we don't need to answer any of your questions fat boy..." Kim opens her mouth, she is furious, "I did this for you Krystal! You came to me that morning and said it happened last night, which is why I went to the school about it, to protect you. Now you're going to lie?" She felt so betrayed.

Now mom is angry we could hear it in her tone of voice, "*KRYSTAL MARIE*! I am so sorry, I think we better go." She grabs me and Krystal by the arm and directs us out the door. Her face looks like she has laser beams coming out of her eyes, her teeth sharp she unlocks the door as we all get in, we know we're in trouble. She starts screaming at me and Krystal about how embarrassed she was and how she didn't teach us to respect adults in that manner. The way home was silent, you could hear a pin drop.

We were finally home and I had never been so thrilled to see my three English Springer Spaniels. They were my babies, my family. I was the only one besides mom who breed, groomed, showed them and whelped the litters. They were AKC Registered and came from Championship lines.

I also showed them around the country with the eye doctor that worked with mom. I noticed a U-Haul in the back driveway, Abby and Matt must be moving out. I think to myself, *YES! The nightmare is finally over.*

Mom instructs us to pack a weeks' worth of clothing that she was taking us out of school the rest of the week and we were staying with Grandma F. We were thrilled; we always loved going to Grandmas'; she was a short Italian woman and your typical old school Italian. As soon as anyone comes in she is always trying to feed them, even though they say no thanks, she is shoving food in their mouth anyway. She always spoiled us, giving us snacks when mom wasn't looking.

The drive was long; about an hour and half. I watched the trees go by; their leaves turning vibrant colors of red, yellow and orange. I think how could there be some much beauty in this world when it seems the evil outweighs the beauty and good. We arrive to see Grandma on the front stoop; she runs down to our car and hugs each of us one by one; tears flowing down her face as if someone had died. She hugged me so hard; I could feel myself gasp for air my lips probably turned blue as she pulled away apologetically. We walked into the house, the aroma was the same as usual, the smell of my grandmother's cooking. She went to the stove to finish cooking her meatballs. Oh how I loved her meatballs.

We all sat down to a wonderful Italian dinner; pasta with homemade sauce, meatballs, pork neck bones, pig skin, salad and Italian bread. My grandfather walks in, he looks at us his face sullen and sits. He is silent. As usual he is served first by my grandmother. It is custom as an Italian wife to take care of her husband and he always comes first before anyone else. I help Grandma clear and clean up after dinner. Chelsea, our aunt whom is only four years older than me goes downstairs to our "hideout." We follow like little ducklings.

After hanging out for a couple of hours and hearing muffled voices; we decide to explore the train set that Grandpa made. It was huge; it had mountains and valleys, cities and towns, urban areas and Indian reservations. The train went round and round and stopped at each station in all the places. We were in awe and amazed. We got distracted by the sudden roar of my grandfather's voice. He was yelling or talking loud;

Italians are known for their loud talking and always mistaken for yelling. Being the protective person I am, I stomp up the basement stairs and into the kitchen I fly. My hands on my hips, looking around the room; I see my mom crying.

"Go back down and play Britt. We are having an adult conversation." She grabs a tissue and blows her nose.

"I will not. I will not stand around and listen to my mother being disrespected. I don't care if it is by your own father." I glare at my grandfather; his mouth opens and before he could say anything I speak in an angry tone looking him right in the eyes. "Mom, you taught us that in order to earn respect you must give respect and right now Grandpa is not showing you any respect." I look at my grandfather trying to keep composed standing straight up like an adult and hold my tears back. "Don't you think that we have been through *ENOUGH* that we don't need any more heart ache from anyone? That we need the loving support from our *FAMILY*!" I walk out of the kitchen leaving the three adults mouths open and silent.

That evening we get settled down in bed. Mom walks in and tucks us in, kisses Kim and Krystal on the cheek and checks on us to make sure were ok. She turns to me smiling. She is looking at me differently now; I can tell she is proud, that she knows she has taught me right. "Britt, I am so proud of you. No one and I mean no one has had the courage that you had tonight to stand up against your grandfather. He will respect you for that. I am so proud of you. I love you so very much. Good night." She kisses my forehead and walks out of the room. "No mo, I am the one who should be proud. Proud to have such a wonderful mother like you." She wipes the tears from her face and closes the door.

Grandma had breakfast already for us in the morning. Grandpa and mom are sitting down already eating and having a nice conversation. I as usual go over to grandma to help and watch her cook. Were sitting down eating breakfast when mom tells us that we're moving in with grandma and grandpa and she will commute to Medford for her job until she finds a new job closer. Kim and Krystal dance around with glee. I sit and look down at my food while playing around with the food with my fork; mom knew I wasn't happy, she sympathized with me It was my junior year and I grew up with those kids and now I would have to start my last two years of high school all over without my childhood friends.....

My grandparents lived in a rich, snooty neighborhood, Upper Brookside, NJ. That meant all the kids thought they were better than everyone else; living in their mansions and mommy and daddy buying them brand new convertibles or mustangs, whichever car was the coolest for that year. That's one thing I loathed. Rich, snotty kids who thought they were better than anyone else; what right do they have?

Things hadn't gone well living with my grandparents, there were constant fights between my mom and grandfather. We were all unhappy. I made some friends in school, pretty much kept to the handful of friends I had and my studies; bringing home A's and B's. Krystal on the other hand was there to socialize as usual. She became popular right away and found all the wrong people. After school she would tell Grandma she was going out to play with some friends.

Time went on, discontent set inside both families. My dad's family didn't want to speak of it at all, while my mom's side did and tried to force my mom to press charges. My mom didn't know what to do; two out of three of her children said the accusations were lies. Kim and I fought which was unusual; she had become a different person. She swore I knew of what was happening that I had participated in some things with her while dad was present. I could not remember anything that happened to me and she called me a liar. I didn't lie, it was the truth I didn't remember anything. The whole house became very hostile and it was decided that Kim go live with Aunt Sophia and Uncle Allen in Beaumont, NJ. She had separated from us like we were the black plague. I felt distressed, embarrassed; me of all people should have known what dad had done to my little sisters'. But why wouldn't they tell me of such a horrific experience. Especially Kim, knowing what I had endured throughout my life as a child/teen. Not only did I lose half a heart, one family but my sister and my best friend. I wish I had known sooner. I was supposed to be there; I was supposed to protect her from the monster that my father had become.

****

The first time we saw our father was eight months later when we had to go to court. Mom had gotten us a new lawyer; at least Krystal and I liked him. Kim pressed charges against our father for what he had done. A lot happened before court. Krystal and I denied the accusations of our father and it made Kim very resentful. There was a lot of fighting between us. Kim had become suicidal and had started therapy; my Aunt got Kim her own lawyer.

Court was finally here. My stomach was in knots; the butterflies wouldn't stop fluttering. I was to be a witness and had to go on stand. Krystal however was a minor and wasn't allowed to go on the stand. I went on the stand and told the truth of how my father had never touched me. After Kim's lawyer cross examined me in which it was a brutal cross examination I was crying as I walked head down to my seat in the back of the court room as we stayed neutral. Kim turned around and looked at me; she glared angrily at me as if I betrayed her and lied. Court went on for two hours and a vital piece of evidence my fathers' lawyer had proved his innocence. The jury too forty-five minutes to deliberate and found him innocent. Kim cried. She told the three of us never to talk, see or contact her ever again. Aunt Sophia and Grandma hugged her in sympathy. My mom walked up to Kim and her family. They turned their backs and walked away. After court we moved back home; my mom's family had disowned us.

Days later, after crying at the loss of a sister and my best friend; we met with our lawyer. He felt for the time being that dad should not live with us for at least one year sober. He was to do Alcoholics anonymous and stick to the program. After that they could talk about supervised visits. We were told we needed to do family counseling to start the healing process. This was court ordered by the judge and to be reviewed one year from the court date to see if he had complied with the judges' orders.

****

A year passed and I was graduating from my old school with all my friends. I couldn't have been happier; my dad was also there to see me graduate. We started our supervised visits with dad; the supervisor appointed by the court was Grandma O and Aunt Jean. We hadn't seen our dad in a year and he welcomed us with open arms. He had been one year sober; I couldn't have been more proud of him. He asked how Kim was doing and we told him what happened after court. I however didn't give up on her. I couldn't. I wrote letter after letter; even though they came back return to sender or no response at all. I am not a quitter and continued to write her. Everything was going fine, our visits with dad continued.

We grew up in a family where my father made it *very clear* that "children should be seen and not heard!" It seemed as thou that was his favorite line besides when we were in trouble and he would say "I brought you into this world, I can take you out." We weren't like kids today; we were not *ALLOWED* to participate in adult conversations. So we were always kicked outside to play with our friends or sent to our rooms to play. There was a lot of loud mumbling coming from the dining room; I decided to open the door slowly and hear what they were yelling or talking about. I heard things like Grandpa O, (my great grandfather) Aunt Dana and Aunt Peggy, my grandma's sister. I didn't know why these names were brought up, nor did I care. Later in my adult years I found out these names were an important vital piece of the puzzle. I slowly closed the door and joined my sisters in playing.

No one in the family spoke of anything that had happened at the trial or about any of the accusations. It was all swept under the carpets by the adults in the family. Tucked away secured and buried deep as if it wasn't to be heard of again. As if my family was trying to hide this dirty secret.......

Chapter Four:

Getting help in therapy

1993

My nightmares started when I was fourteen. They were mostly the same dreams; a black figure that I couldn't identify chasing me. Sometime it would catch me and do horrible things to me; take advantage of me; I'd scream and nothing would come out, and things such as kill me, cut me from my chest to my stomach and etc... They were very vivid and seemed so real. I remember saying to myself, praying in my nightmares to wake up, sometimes even pinching myself to see if it was real. I'd wake up screaming and in cold sweats. Mom would rush in to see if I was Ok. I never really told her what my dreams were about just that I had been having nightmares and they seemed so real; as if I felt the blade of the knife pierced through my skin and that it felt so real. I told her how at first it was one black figure then it was two to three and sometimes a fourth would show up, I always felt trapped with nowhere to go. Some nights I'd wake up hyperventilating and couldn't breathe. Mom talked to our family doctor and told him how I've been having awful nightmares and was afraid to go to sleep and wasn't sleeping anymore. He told her to try melatonin over the counter and if after a month that doesn't work try Valerian root. He said if neither works then he would have to prescribe me sleeping pills.

My mom tried everything to prevent me from going on sleeping pills. She even consulted her sister who was a doctor. She tried everything; I was just too scared to sleep. I was terrified; petrified to see the black figures, scared to run from them only to be caught and die in my sleep over and over again. It was to the point where even if I was awake I'd see the figures when I closed my eyes. I was haunted; I felt trapped. Mom spoke to our Doctor and made me an appointment. I explained everything to him. He prescribed me Ambien for sleep. I cried and screamed *NO* as I ran out of the office. After a lengthy conversation between mom and the doctor, he suggested I do therapy with the possibility of hypnosis along with taking the Ambien. Mom agreed.

1996

The room had a light smell of gardenia mixed with lavender. Josie, my therapist knew those were my two favorite smells; of course she knew me quite well by now. I had been in therapy for almost three years now. I always burn incense of Gardenia's and lavender in my room; especially when I smoked pot. They always covered the smell real well. They helped me relax and put me at ease and calmed me. The room was huge, Victorian style with cathedral ceilings and paintings of angels, clouds and the sun shining brightly. The couches and chairs were made of velour and were so comfortable. Josie, (who insisted we be on a first name basis) decided along with myself that it was time to try going into deep hypnosis and into my dreams to figure out who or what these black figures were. I was frightened, she could tell by the expression on my face. I was terrified my secret would come out and she would tell my parents as I am a minor. I wasn't sure if three years of therapy I was ready for this point of my life.

"Britt, I've told you from the beginning of our sessions that I cannot and will not disclose any information or what we discuss with anyone you don't want me to. It is my job that would be on the line. You can trust me. Here you can know this is your safe haven and no harm can come of you. Are you sure that you are ready for this?"

My face turned white and I looked down, my hands and fingers are fidgeting. I take a deep breath and in a soft voice "Yes, yes I'm ready Josie."

"Ok lie down on the couch and get comfortable. I want you to close your eyes and clear your mind. Listen to nothing but my voice. First thing is Britt; we need to establish a safe word and a happy place for you. The safe word is a word that you will remember when we've gone too far into your dreams and it frightens you too much you tell me your safe word and I will redirect you to your happy place and wake you up. Your safe word can be a color, a name, a pet, a car, anything that you know you can remember quickly so I can get you out and redirect you. Does that sound like a plan? Does that put you at ease Britt?"

"Yes it does. I just have to think on the word….. Hmm, how about Red for stop. It's easy, red=stop."

"Red, that's the perfect word. Great now close your eyes. I want you to familiarize your safe word. I want you to say it over and over in your head. Listen to your words, feel the comfort and ease it puts you. Feel that it makes you safe… Now I want you to envision a safe place; a place full of peace, serenity, something that makes you happy. I want you to thinks of the smells, your surroundings. What's around you that comforts you that puts you at ease. A place no one would even know about; only you and I. I want you to keep your eyes closed and take in the smells, the sounds, your surroundings, what would be in your safe place."

"I am in a meadow full of gardenias and lilacs, the sun is shining bright and I hear the blue jays chirping. The smell of the fresh gardenias and lilacs soothe my inner soul. I see butterflies. A lot of butterflies; it's like a garden of them. They are fluttering from flower to flower; some are flying around me and land on me. Their wings tickle my neck and nose and I giggle. I am running through the meadow laughing, just like I'm a little girl again. I see something blue up ahead and hear rushing water."

"Walk towards it Britt, this is your happy place no harm will come of you."

"I am walking towards it. Oh it's beautiful. It a pond, crystal blue. I can see all the way to the bottom. There are beautiful, vibrant colorful fish in the pond. To the right of it is a waterfall; Oh, it must be Fifteen feet high! The sound of the rushing water cascading down between the bright green foliage relaxes me and make me feel safe."

"That is very good Britt. I want you to keep your happy place tucked safely in your mind. Try not to dream of it as you may make it vulnerable to your predators."

"I feel free!!! I feel safe!!! Like no one can ever hurt me again!"

"Now that we have your safe place established and your safe word; I'd like to try some exercises before we go into your dreams just to make sure you have the control to say your safe word and get redirected to your happy place. Britt, what is your safe word again?"

"Red." I said unsure; my mind distracted from the beauty of my safe place. If only I could stay here forever….

"Excellent! Now let's practice. You ready?"

"As ready as I'll ever be….

****

1993-1995

Mom and the three of us were on our way to our first day of therapy. The three of pouting and sulking in the back seat. I watched out the window as we traveled up I29 towards Mecca, NY. I immersed my thoughts to the beauty of the fall foliage. The mountains always looked glorious this time of year with their vibrant colors of yellows, reds and oranges. I thought to myself why mom couldn't find a therapist closer to home. A very annoyed and whiny Krystal speaks up and talks fast "Are we there yet? Why do we need therapy, I don't think I need therapy, really mom?! We really don't need therapy."

Krystal always annoyed us when she opened up her mouth as a child. She was always whiny and annoying. She always wanted what she wanted when she wanted it and she always got it. Mom always catered to her; of course she was the baby. So she was always spoiled by mom. Kim and I always thought mom just gave her what she wanted half the time just to shut her up. Kim and I looked at Krystal and rolled our eyes. You could tell by mom's tone of voice that she was annoyed. This had been Krystal's sixth time asking. "Yes, we are fifteen minutes away. You girls will really like Josie. I have already met with her as well as your dad several times now.

Also your Aunt Jean was a student under her when she was studying child psychology. She had nothing bad to say about her and said that you all would love her. Let's give it a try for one month and if by then you feel the same way I promise you won't have to go anymore." We all looked at each other and nodded.

I hated going to Mecca. There was so much crime and though I am not racist nor ever have mocked anyone's religion; Mecca was 75% of Hassidic Jews. Their odor filled the air on the streets and it made me gag every time. We turn down an alleyway; it gave me a creepy feeling as I slide my hand over locking my door and gesturing to Kim to do the same. I had always had this sick feeling about things. Mom called it a gift. She had the same thing. We could pick up on certain things our guts tell us as well as people's emotions and feel how they feel; it affects our own mood, as if we absorb their emotions. At the end of the alley way we make a left and proceed to go straight to a dead end. I am puzzled at the dead end and right in front of us is a beautiful Victorian house; off white with coffee colored shutters and trim. I was in awe. I loved Victorian houses and had hoped that someday I would own one of my own. We travel up the hill on the right side of the circular driveway; there is a sign that says one way. As we get up closer I see beautiful gardens of flowers and beautifully cut shrubs into different figures, animals and shapes; just like art. In front of the house there is parking. Mom parks the car and gets out. The three of us just stare, frozen like an ice statue, hearts beating out of our chests. Mom gestures to us to get out of the car and taps her watch. We all reluctantly get out of the car.

We walk in to this huge room which I assumed was the waiting room. A middle aged lady about 5'1"maybe shorter, she was a little on the heavy side with brown curly hair. She comes out of the room to the left of us. She has a very pleasant, warming smile and a comforting, motherly feeling about her. She introduces herself and insists that we call her by her first name Josie. She said when we call her "Mrs. Smith" she looks around for her mother-in-law. We were always taught to be respectful and to address adults by their last name or mam/sir. She guided us to this huge room. It was so beautiful and huge. I had always dreamt of having a house with an exact room like this. I felt at ease, I could only speak for myself as I notice my sisters' body language they were not pleased at all to be here. I am sure they will not be cooperative.

Josie speaks softly "Please sit down wherever you would like and feel more comfortable." Krystal chooses this red velour chair in on corner of the room, while Kim chooses the flowered love seat in the opposite corner of the room. Both had pouty faces and arms folded. "This is stupid!" Krystal shouts out. Mom looks at her and gives her a dirty look and mouths something that looks "like lose the attitude." "Krystal that is very good, it's how you feel, now tell me why you feel that way." Krystal is silent staring at Josie. She doesn't say a peep just stares. Josie looks at Krystal, then Kim and lastly me. "It's ok if you don't want to share. I won't make you do anything you don't want to, just so you girls know, it is court ordered that you all receive family and individual therapy until I sign you all off when completed."

We all sit in silence; you could hear a pin drop. Krystal struggles to get comfortable in her chair, a normal nervous reaction she has. Kim lies down in the love seat looking at her nails ignoring what Josie had to say. I, myself looks around the room and take all the beauty of the room inside me. I have only experienced ugliness in my childhood, it's nice to see some good and beauty still exists. The artwork is beautiful it fills the room. I notice a painting in the far side of the room. No way is it a Renoir? I get up to get a better look at it. It is! It is! Renoir is my favorite painter; I actually own five of his paintings but not this one. I look at it and get entranced in the beauty of the painting. Everything and everyone disappears; it's me and the painting. I never heard a thing; I feel a tap on my shoulder and my trance is broken; all too often I daydream. Take myself to a place where there is no bad only good in my world. "Britt, we have called you five times. Why didn't you respond?" "I'm sorry mom, you know me and Renoir paintings, I guess I just got lost in it and was in a daze. I'm very sorry." I sit back down with mom on the couch across from Josie. She asks if any of us wanted to do one on one therapy, we shook our heads except for mom. Mom asked us to sit in the waiting room while she spoke with Josie.

The way home no one said a word. When we got home we all went to our rooms. Mom comes to my room and peeks in, "May I come in and talk to you?" "Sure." Mom looks around, "Did you rearrange your room again?" I am constantly changing the furniture around in my room at least once, sometimes twice a week. I don't know why, it started when I was fourteen and became an insomniac. My room was the only thing I had control of. "Yea, you know me." "Well with dad gone I'm going to need your help with the girls and around the house." I thought to myself, well no duh what do you think I have been doing all my life. Did you actually believe dad was that responsible to do everything himself? "Of course, anything you need mom. I'm here for you always." A tear rolls down her face, "Thank you Britt." She gets up and walks slowly out of my room and into hers. I think to myself and wonder how hard this situation must be for her, how much pain and heartache. She doesn't deserve any of this.

Mom and the three of us continue therapy with Josie twice a week. The first session of the week was family therapy and after two years were able to see dad again and he was involved in our family therapy. We didn't know but he too had been seeing Josie the past two years. The second session of the week was our individual therapy sessions. Kim and Krystal had finally opened up and became cooperative. During one of our family sessions after court; a huge fight between Kim and Dad broke out, this is what prompted mom and Josie to agree that she live with mom's sister for awhile and seek therapy down there.

Three years go by and dad had celebrated his three year anniversary of being sober at AA. We were all invited. Mom and dad's mom went back to the courts to prove his sobriety and therapy to get the supervised visits lifted. Shortly after he moved back in with us. Krystal and I had seen a different side of him; he seemed more loving, fun, concerned and more involved. We were proud but confused by this change in him; we were not used to it but loved it. I continue to write to Kim and my letters still came back return to sender or never came back at all with no response. Being the person I am I still kept writing her; I was never a quitter.

1996

For weeks, Josie and I practiced my safe word in different scenarios to help me get redirected to my happy place until she became comfortable that I had the power to use my safe word and redirect myself to my happy place. "Very good Britt, you have come a long way and have improved very much. Next session we will visit your dreams, that's if you are comfortable with that." I nodded my head. "Great I will see you next week."

The next session came quickly; it seemed like only yesterday I had my session and was practicing my safe word. Krystal went for her session first. I sat in the waiting room anxiously waiting. My palms were sweaty; my heart was beating out of my chest. I stood up and started walking back and forth fidgeting with my fingers; I was nervous about this particular session. I walked over to the water and got myself a cool cup and guzzled it down the filled it up again and drank that cup quickly as well. I started pacing again when my mom looked at me and spoke "Britt, will you please sit down your making me a nervous wreck." She was agitated, "Sorry mom." Krystal came out of the room, wow that went by fast. What was thirty minutes long it seemed to be five minutes. Josie looked at me and waved me in, she smiled warmly at me.

"Make yourself comfortable Britt. Are you sure you're ready for this? I don't want to make you do anything you don't want to, especially if you're not ready." She must've sensed my fear, my panic, how nervous I was. She glanced down at my shirt; my fingers were twirling it around, pulling and prodding it. I hadn't noticed she never missed any body language. "You're going to rip a hole in that shirt my dear." "Oh. No, I am ready just a bit nervous. Isn't that a normal feeling for this type of therapy?" "You're right, it is. Sometimes it can be dangerous or more damaging to a person. You need to know this. This is why for two months I had practiced with you on your safe word and redirecting you to your happy place. These tools are very vital to your hypnosis. Without them it can be dangerous or damaging. But if you feel you need more practice or are not ready that if ok. We can continue to practice. The choice is yours." "No, I'm ready, let's do this."

"Ok, I want you to lie down, get comfortable, and feel at ease… Fix the pillows so you're nice and relaxed; fix them the way you like. Are you comfortable?" I nod my head. "Great. Close your eyes. I want you to listen to the sound of my voice, hear how soft and gentle I'm talking. Clear your mind, all you can hear is the sound of my voice in the emptiness. Nod your head if you hear my voice in the emptiness of your head." I nod. "Good Britt, now remember no matter what when I snap my fingers you will awaken. Do you understand? Repeat back to me." I speak softly, tiredly "No matter what you snap your fingers I will be awake." "Good. Now Brittney one more important thing, what is your safe word?" My mind is empty as I struggle to say my safe word. Finally in a tired zombie like voice I say "Red." "Excellent. Let's begin…."

"Brittney, I'd like you to take me to your happy place. Tell me about it."

"I am in my meadow. I can smell the fresh scents of gardenia and lilacs. In the far distance I hear the birds chirping and the waterfall beating down into the crystal blue pond. I fall back and feel the warmth of the sun beating down on my face and body. I am awoken by the tickling of my feet, neck and face from the fluttering butterfly. I giggle; I feel like a kid. Here I can be a kid."

"Britt, it's beautiful. This is a wonderful, tranquil and serene happy place. Do you see way past the pond, at the end of the meadow there is a dirt road?"

"Yes. I see the dirt road. But I didn't put that in my happy place."

"No you didn't, but that is the road into your dreams and at the end of it is the door to enter them. Let's go follow the road, I am here with you."

"Ok." I say hesitantly. I walk slowly, looking behind me to find my crutch, Josie. She has disappeared. I panic. "Josie, JOSIE!" "Britt, I am still with you but this is something you need to do yourself but know I am here." I nod my head and proceed to the door. The door was huge and appeared to be out of the Middle Ages; strong wooden door with metal bolts and a wooden 6x4 plank that is set in iron for me to push up and remove to open. Above the door in big, black, capital letters spell the word DREAMS. The middle of the door was an in scripture in red that said RED. My safe word…. I say it over and over in my head so I don't forget when I enter my dreams. I slowly open the door as it creaks, I peek around the door slowly expecting the worst….

It is pitch black, I can't see a thing. I start to panic, my breathing quickens as I feel the darkness overwhelm me. There is a light ahead; thank goodness. I put my arms out to balance myself walking down the hallway towards the light. There are no walls; I bend down and feel if the floor leads up to the walls. Maybe they're further apart than I thought. What! I start crying the floor is about four feet wide and beyond that is emptiness…. Fear sets in as I race straight for the light trying to run in a straight line as not to fall into the bottomless pit. I break through the light and look around. This looks all too familiar, it's my dream; I feel like a kid again. I become giddy, running around and spinning before dropping to the ground. This is the only time I can feel like a kid, my dreams. My happiness ends when I feel an overwhelming sense of terror blanket my body. I feel the warmth of someone's breath against the back of my neck. The hairs on my arm stand straight up as I freeze. My mouth tries to scream my safe word but nothing comes out. I start to run glancing back behind me only to find a black figure running after me almost catching up to me. I find my voice and scream *"RED! RED!"*

I hear a faint voice in the distance and start running as fast as I can towards it. The faster I run the louder I hear it. A woman's voice is calling my name.

"Britt, I want you to take a breath and breathe in through your nose. Smell the fresh air. You smell the sweet succulent aroma of Lilacs and Gardenias. The birds are chirping, off in the distance you see your meadow and garden of butterflies. Run to them Britt."

I look behind me; I am surrounded by Gardenias and Lilacs. I am relieved, my racing heart begins to slow down, and the fear is starting to dissipate. I hear the roaring of my waterfall and the rushing pond. I am at my safe place. I am awoken by the snap of Josie's fingers. "I watched your fear and your struggle. I wanted to direct you to your happy place, but you needed to let me know when enough was enough. Tell me…. What happened? What did you see?" I proceeded to tell her of my horrific experience and how real it felt to me. She reassured me that this was my choice and if I felt I couldn't handle it or didn't want to do it I didn't have to. I told her I needed closure for myself and needed to know why. I needed to sleep and not worry if I'm going to be scared to death to close my eyes.

We continued hypnosis every week and every week a little bit of the puzzle came to light. Now faces of two of the shadows were blurred but I still could not figure who they were. Over time we came to know that the shadows were; Pete and Matt. I told Josie how I never told anyone but Kim. I never reported the sexual assault to the cops. I left it be. That was how I dealt with everything; just push it deep inside and cover it with a ton of bricks so it could never surface.

"Britt that is so unhealthy to hold such trauma as what you have been through inside. I'm glad you told me, but we should really discuss this further in detail. If you really want closure you need to do this." I shook my head intently. "Ok, I won't push you."

We completed therapy when I was seventeen. Josie and I never found out who that third black figure was. She said it may be a possibility if Kim was right on her accusations; that it could be dad and since I had such a traumatic childhood I could have repressed those memories so far I don't recollect a single incident. I didn't believe that could be but left it as that. The most important tool I got from Josie was the power to be able to control my nightmarish dreams. She taught me how to redirect myself to my happy place while I was having a nightmare. Every since therapy, I had one nightmare. Until later on in my adult years, but that is another story.

Chapter Five:

Al-Anon and Al-Ateen

1993

Josie suggested that since my dad was in Alcoholics Anonymous (AA) that mom should try out an Al-Anon meeting. She felt it would give her a better understanding of the alcoholic and those they love whom they affect. Josie wrote down a list of churches in Medford that she may stop by and see if they have any Al-Anon support groups.

For anyone who doesn't know what Al-Anon is, let me explain to you what this support group is that changed my life and outlook on my father. *"Al-Anon Family groups are a fellowship of relatives and friends of alcoholics who share their experience, strength and hope in order to solve their common problem. It is believed that alcoholism in the family is an illness and that changed attitudes can aid recovery."*) * "Al-Anon has one purpose but to help families of alcoholics and help them understand their disease and our own mishaps. We do this by practicing the Twelve Steps and using their tools to manage our everyday lives."*

Mom found a group in Lockney; it was pretty close to home. She enjoyed the company of her newly found friends and Al-Anon Family, but most of all she felt comfortable with them, she trusted them. The meetings were the first Tuesday and the third Thursday evenings at 7:00 at the Lockney Christian Church. Mom never missed one meeting; she became so serious about this program.

She had what they would call a sponsor (A.K.A. Mentor) to help the newcomer work on their Twelve Step program. She was all about working the program; but you know what? She was the biggest enabler in the family! I have made her known that too.

****

1996

Saturday's I usually had to be up by Seven am, dad always said "you're going to sleep the day away if you sleep past Seven am." Had to start my chores before I could go play with my friends. It was a beautiful sunny, breezy glorious day. Mom is frantically sweeping off our three tier twenty-four foot by eighteen foot deck my dad and I built from the bottom up. He designed it and together we built it. He always joked that I was the son he never had. I took an interest in manual labor, building things, chopping/stacking wood, working on cars with him, fixing up his Demo Derby cars with him, etc…

She catches a glimpse of me out of the corner of her eye and sounding all frazzled she breathed out "Oh good Britt you're up. I need help. I have so much to do today and all in six hours."

Great I think, must be another last minute BBQ I think to myself as I roll my eyes. "What do you need Mo (*my nickname for her*)?" Mom rattled everything off so quick all I heard was "Blah blah blah blah blah blah blah BLAH" I knew exactly what she wanted done. Clean the whole house, straighten out the deck and start setting up. I had *ESP*, who knew!

Three hours passed by I had everything all cleaned and set up, mo pulls in honking her horn four times signaling her daughters to come out and unload the car. Looking all discombobulated; mom speaks breathless "Britt, we (pauses to catch her breath) have to prepare the food. Can you help me please?"

"Of course Mo." I had a puzzled look on my face, "Um Mo, what's going on? Are we having a BBQ?" She looks at me, her eyes darkened from lack of sleep and drained from work. I can tell how exhausted she was. "Yea just a few family, you know the usual and I invited my sponsor from Al-Anon and his wife." I think to myself oh now I know why she is all frazzled and has to have everything so perfect, her sponsor is coming for the first time. She always told us first impressions are what people base their opinions on you.

"Mo why don't you go take a relaxing hot, bubble bath and relax for a bit. Tell me what you need me to prepare and I will do it." Mom hugs me and smiles softly. She rattles off what needs to be done and disappears into her room.

****

It was about one-thirty pm, Mo's sponsor and wife had already arrived on time and were sitting at our octagonal table my dad and I built. They had been talking about Al-Anon and working on the Step program. Our family as usual was always fashionably late. We always joked that they would be late for their own funeral. Mo signals me to come over. She introduces me to her sponsor and his wife. Children and teens cannot join Al-Anon as you need to be 18 to join.

"Britt this is Daren, my sponsor from Al-Anon and his wife Carol." I put my hand out and smile warmly as I shake both their hands professionally. My dad always said you should always give a nice firm handshake and look people in the eyes when you do. It gives you character and is professional. "Very nice to meet the both of you." Daren and his wife reciprocate. "Britt, Daren was just telling me how he is the group leader for the Al-Ateen group at the same church on Wednesday evenings at five pm. He and I both agree it would benefit both you and Krystal to understand your father as an alcoholic and how it's a disease and controls the person."

My face drops, everyone looks at me eyes wide open. I am silent; I don't know what to say. I think I don't want to do this. "Wow, that's not what I expected to hear. I will discuss this with Krystal and we'll let Mo know." I power walk away heading for the sliding glass door closing it as I hear my mom yell for me.

****

It was our first Al-Ateen meeting, Mo made sure we got there early to help Daren set up. We entered the church at the back and through two metal creaky doors that slammed behind us. It made me jump out of my skin. I was nervous, not knowing what was going to go on at this meeting and having a room full of strangers. My heart races, I get anxiety when I meet new people or don't know anyone. I think to myself boy I need a joint about now. We walk down the cellar stars and see Daren. He is a skinny, tall man with salt and pepper hair, a very nice gentleman. His voice is mono toned and could put a whole room to sleep. Krystal however had always made fun of people she didn't know, it's always the person she had always been. Just like my Aunt Josie she was the light of the party. She was comical and vibrant. She didn't care what she said to anyone, there was no filter on her mouth. We always said she could win an Academy award for her antics. We say Hi to Daren and automatically mo tells him that we are early to help him set up. Krystal whispers a few choice words into my ear that I was relived she didn't say out loud. We finished setting the table in a circle as Daren proceeds to explain the reason why we have the chairs in a circle.

"The circle signifies our never-ending Al-Ateen family, we are all equal in here. Regardless if you're a newcomer or if you've been here for a year or more. The circle reminds us that as a group no one can break the bond between us as our Al-Ateen Family." I smile and nod. I look around the room, it looks similar to a classroom and desks are against the wall with our chairs in the middle of the room. The room was smelled murky, it had ugly brown indoor/outdoor carpeting and the walls were an ugly yellowish tan color. Not quite too inviting or captivating. On the walls were artwork, I walk up to them as I await for others to arrive. They are pictures with sayings of hope and recovery. Some say *"One day at a time, Let Go, Let God, I cannot control the alcoholic but I can control how I handle* *the situation".*)* Some of the artworks were very intriguing and the words made me ponder awhile.

It's five o'clock pm and kids start pouring in. Krystal and I are already sitting playing with our thumbs waiting nervously. We think, do we know anyone? A familiar face walks in. It is a friend of Krystal's and the brother of a friend of mine. A sigh of relief passes through us. Jessie takes a seat next to us. "Thank goodness I finally know someone here. I've been coming for a few weeks now and was becoming hopeless." Daren clears his throat signaling the meeting was starting. The room becomes silent. We start by holding each other's hand and closing our eyes while bowing our heads saying *"Let it Begin With Me... When anyone, anywhere, reaches out for help. Let the hand of Al-Anon and Al-Ateen always be there and Let it Begin With me.")** Krystal and I mumble the words we aren't too familiar with as everyone says it in tune with Darren. Daren starts with the girl to the right of him asking her if she had anything new she would like to share. She speaks of how her mother is an alcoholic and how it has affected her in so many different ways. It's made her frustrated and angry. Something I can relate to. I catch a glimpse of Krystal rolling her eyes and whispering to Jessie. "Shhhh. Listen Krystal. You might learn something." She sticks her tongue out at me and sits up in her chair with attitude. I glare at her. Daren goes around the room in order. Listening to all the kids experiencing what my sister's and I have been put through made me ponder my life and the tragedy I have faced. Not only could I use these tools for the alcoholism that has taken prisoner of not only my father but half of my family as well; but everything I have endured throughout my childhood. It came to be my turn and I regretfully decline to speak as does Krystal. Daren pulls out an orange book with a sun on it. I couldn't make out the words except for Al-Ateen. "I want everyone to take out their Al-Ateen Hope for Children of Alcoholics and turn to page four. Krystal and Britt here are your books to keep." We both thank him and turn to the page. "Britt, would you please read the first paragraph?" I swallow and clear my throat. Why me, I think. I proceed to read the first paragraph as he calls on the next person for the last paragraph. The next paragraph is today's reminder, a quote. Daren reads the quote. *"Sharing experiences widens one's horizons and opens out new and better ways to deal with difficulties. There is no need to solve them* *alone."*)* "Your homework for next week. I want you to analyze this quote and in your own words explain what this means to you. I want you to be creative and take the time to think and reflect on this. It should be at least 2-3 paragraphs long or more if you'd like. I will pick the top three and the winners will get a special dinner with me and my wife." The room was in awe and everyone wowed.

It was time to go, Mo was waiting outside in the car for us. "So? How'd it go?" Krystal rolled her eyes, "*BORING!*" I turn around and look at her, "Well if you paid attention maybe you wouldn't of been bored and actually learn something. It was ok, I learned some things." Mo looked at me and smiled.

Mo drove us two more times and then I started to drive us to meetings. Everything was going good, we were attending our meetings regularly and mo let us go get a slice of pizza with Jessie afterwards. We had so much fun with Jessie and it was exciting skipping our meeting, so much that we started skipping every meeting. Being as our group leader was Mo's sponsor that was short lived and she didn't make us go, she didn't want to force us to do anything.

Krystal was a very stubborn, snobbish, I'm better than you out of control teenager. She too started smoking Marijuana with me when she was twelve years old. I remember when mom wasn't home the two of us would invite our stoner friends over to get high with us. We always had the best times being stoned with them.

Krystal was the complete opposite of me in every way. She was a social butterfly in school, not caring about her learning and bringing home C's-F on her report card. Really, she was there for the social aspect of school. While I was there to learn and kept my GPA up so I could go to college. She was an out of control teen, sneaking out of the house late at night to see Mark; I, myself never had the nerve to do such a thing. She dropped out of school when she was in the tenth grade at sixteen years old. When my father had heard of this and caught her sneaking out he flipped out. She hated when people tried to control her life; she felt only she had the right to do and have the say over what she does. He threatened and said "As long as your under my roof young lady, you will follow my rules!" "*FINE!*"

Krystal screams at him and storms into the kitchen and rustles trough the cabinet and stomps down the hallway. We hear her slam the door. Angrily, my father stomps after her with my mom crying and whimpering behind. The door is locked. He starts banging on the door, *"Open this door RIGHT NOW KRYSTAL MARIE!"* I hear the door unlock, Krystal is filling large black garbage bags with clothes and all her stuff. She yells, "I cannot stay with your stupid ridiculous rules! I am leaving!" Mo cries, screaming at her, "Noooo Krystal please! Your way too young! *PLEASE DON'T* leave!" "Sorry mom, I just can't stay here anymore." She Walks out the door.

****

She met her high school sweetheart, Mark in fifth grade and they were inseparable until they were twenty-five when Krystal's drug habit went spiraling out of control due to him. Mark dropped out of school in the ninth grade the year before Krystal and went to work with his grandfather and cousin in the families' tree business. Krystal was doing great on her own, as we knew. She only showed us what she wanted us to see. She had her own apartment and waitressed at a diner 5 days a week as well as picking up bartending shifts at the Honky Tonk Bar & Restaurant from Thursdays through Sundays. In 2 years Mo bought the Optical business from her boss and went into business with the Optometrist they had. She asks Krystal to come work for her full-time as her Optician. I was her first choice as I was more mature and reliable than Krystal. At the time I wasn't available to work with Mo, I had been working at Wal-Mart as a Manager.

It was awhile before I noticed that Krystal had a drinking problem. I always thought Why? Did she not see what we went through with dad? Yea he was sober for five years now, so what was her excuse? I've learned a life lesson from him and family for that I am grateful.

It had been four years since I was in Al-Ateen and then I didn't take it seriously, I was a teenager. I did remember some things I had read. I decided to go on the internet and find some Al-Anon groups in the area that I could attend on lunch breaks or before/after work. It took about three groups for me to feel comfortable with the people and feel like I actually fit in. I found a sponsor and started my step work. I tried to impress but not force AA on Krystal, but only share my experience and excitement in my newly found discoveries in Al-Anon. She gave me a disgusted look. She seemed like a lost cause…..

"Some people don't know how badly they need a new way of life until disaster overtakes them.")*

Chapter Six:

Getting help and hope for an Aunt

Growing up it was always the norm for us children for both sides of our families to drink alcohol. On my mother's side we had a 100% Italian family. It was always custom to have wine with dinner. Holidays we has wine and Asti Spumante (Champagne), even the children got a little 3oz wine glass for dinners and holidays. Holidays in the Italian household was very hectic, Grandma would be up at three am cooking, when I woke up I'd be right by her side helping. I'd always watch her cook with all the different liquors', red and white wines. She would always pour herself a 6 oz glass of Vermouth as she cooked. By the time dinner was ready Grandma would already be drunk.

After dinner "the children" had to clear the tables and clean up the dinner dishes. We minded, but not so much….. We did what we had to do leaving the glasses for last, they were so delicate, we didn't want to break them loading them in the dishwasher with the heavy stuff. We would line the glasses up on the counter empty to the back and glasses with champagne or wine towards the front. Then each of us would share and drink the remainder of the contents in each glass. We got giddy, happy and wobbly. By the end of the night all my Aunts, Uncles, mom, grandma and us kids were all drunk.

My father's side of the family Alcoholism seemed to run in the family as well as some drug addiction. Never my Grandmother, she was always like a saint; it's why I never understood how the majority of her five children where Alcoholics and/or drug addicts. My Grandmother was always very serious on her Catholicism, she was a very active parishioner in her church. She volunteered for everything and was a Sunday school teacher. It started with my father, as you may well know from chapter one; he was a alcoholic and drug addict.

The next in line was my Aunt Dana; she had Juvenile Diabetes from birth. We've heard from everyone about how beautiful she was. How her light brown hair glistened in the sun and her big brown eyes twinkled like the stars. How I wish she was around long enough to get to know her more than I did.

My father and her could not stand each other, but hung with the same crowd and went to the same parties. She too was an Alcoholic and a drug addict. I don't remember much about her when I was younger, except she adored us girls so much and she was my cousin Jake's mom. Jake was a year younger than me and a year older than Kim. As I got older, the alcohol and drugs took a hold on her having the Juvenile diabetes. Little by little my Aunt's limbs had to be cut off. She didn't care she kept going until she died at the younger age of thirty years old. I remember being afraid and horrified, we all were, especially Jake.

The third child of my grandmother's was my Godfather Uncle Jim. He drank Alcohol, but didn't get carried away with it. He was an engineer in the United States Air force.

Aunt Deb was Grandma's fourth child. She is an Alcoholic. A very *BIG CLOSET* Alcoholic. I say "*is an Alcoholic*" because it is a disease and even though someone may be in sobriety they are still considered an alcoholic. They still have tendencies. Tell me if you train a cat not to eat and starve that cat then wave a mouse in front of it, would the cat go for it? Ponder that question for a moment. My guess is; is that that cat's will is fragile, weak and will go for that mouse. That cat is my Aunt Deb.

I remember how fun and hysterical it was for us kids; the three of us along with our two cousins Jake and Keith to follow Aunt Deb around with her 24oz coke bottle fill ¼ way with coke and ¾'s with Vodka. We'd sneak and follow her to see where she'd hide her next bottle. It was like a game to us. She would be drunk by the end of the night and none of the adults knew how she got drunk. But we kids knew how, we would always giggle. It was the highlight of the holidays for us.

Eventually after all the adults exhausted their ideas on where she would hide the bottles, we came into play. Chanting, singing and giggling in harmony, we all skipped hand in hand leading the adults to Aunt Deb's secret hiding spots. No one would have ever guessed her spots had it not been for us sneaking following her. She hid bottles in the shed all the way up in the rafters. She dug holes in the garden and buried them.

The front porch was built with concrete, well the bottom left section behind the hedges has an eight inch by six inch section that had crumbled apart and she had hollowed it out and replaced the hole with bricks. Not only was she an Alcoholic but she was a smart Alcoholic. The adults gathered all the evidence, eight bottles worth, it's a wonder how she's still breathing. They confronted her so many times, it would always end the same way; Aunt Deb walking out the door and walking to the nearest bar.

My Aunt Deb had nothing to lose, no husband, no children and no house. She lived with my Great Grandmother in the apartment attached to Grandma O's house. She was very close to her Grandmother, helping her and doing what she needed. When she passed my Aunt went off the deep end; ending up drunk for her wake and funeral making a mockery of herself in front of hundreds of people. After her death, Aunt Deb went spiraling out of control. Aunt Deb knew she needed help due to the many interventions our family had on her. But the most influential person that had the most impact on her was her oldest brother, my father. He had been in sobriety for seven years and doing excellent. She would call him constantly spending hours upon end on the phone with him, trying to gain his support and encouraging words. You can support and encourage an alcoholic or drug addict but you cannot force them into sobriety. They have to want it, they need to be ready and they need to "hit Rock Bottom" as all the programs say. Aunt Deb wasn't ready, she hadn't hit her Rock bottom yet.

Late one evening we received a call. Dad answered the phone. We here him in a calming voice speaking to a very scared and frantic person, "Ok, calm down Deb. I can't understand a word your saying. Speak slowly and calmly." He pauses to listen, his facial expression turns to anger then to sympathy. "I am on my way, you stay where you are and don't you move. I'm coming to get you. *WHAT!* You're walking on Interstate 77 are you looking for a death wish? Go to the rest stop and stay there! I'm leaving now!" I never saw my dad move so quickly, grabbed his jacket and ran out the door yelling to Mo "I'll explain when we get back." He peeled out of the driveway. The drive is a three hour long round trip to where Aunt Deb was so I knew dad would be home very late, Kim, Krystal and I went to bed.

The way home Aunt Deb explained to dad that she was at Jim's drinking. She met a guy named Frankie and he kept buying her drinks. She was flattered and moneyless so she accepted his offer. She was about to leave and walk home when Freddie offered to walk her home or to the end of her block. She was impressed and thought what a nice gentlemen. They talked, they laughed and then Freddie kissed her. It took her by surprise as she pushed away telling him she doesn't want to get involved. Long story short, he beat the crap out of her and left her on the sidewalk bleeding and curled up in a ball. When cops saw her on the sidewalk they tried to approach her. "Mam', are you ok?" She gets up turning so the cops don't see her face and proceed to walk slowly, "I am fine officer, just needed to rest a bit and I took a long walk and didn't realize it was so long." "Ok just checking. We try to keep Woodbury as safe as possible." She nodded and went on her way walking to the rest stop at I-77. Dad laid some rules down and instructed her that absolutely NO alcohol is to be brought into our house or she is never to be drunk in his house. They will also find a good reputable long-term recovery center to help her get sober. Until they could get her into one and she obeyed his rules she was welcomed to stay with them as long as she was enrolled into a program.

It took us two weeks and a lot of research on the internet and word of mouth to find a successful recovery center called The Caring Recovery Center. It is a long term program depending on how well you do. No one ever leaves before a year at least. Some are there for 2-5 years. They have a 98% success rate. The center was an hour away in Montway, NY. Dad, Mo and I brought her to her newly founded home, it was bittersweet. I told Aunt Deb how proud of her I was on cooperating with her recovery and I wish her well. I promised her I would be there for her for support and encouragement; she could always count on me. Aunt Deb grabbed me and held me tight.

The forty-five minute ride was pleasant, Aunt Deb and I had wonderful conversations as we traveled down beautiful country roads before we go into the city of Mecca, NY. The vibrant colors of reds, yellows and oranges seemed to light up as the sun shone brightly behind them. I was in awe at the beauty of it all, as was Aunt Deb. I told her how proud I was of her for taking this first step to her recovery and I would be there for here any time she needed me, whether it was just to talk, cry, and breakdown, I'd be her #1 cheerleader. I told her about how much I had learned in Al-Anon and told her that the road to recovery wasn't going to be so easy for her, but if she felt weak or felt like she needed "that drink" call me immediately and I would help her get through it all.

We arrive to the caring center and pulled into the parking lot. There was a big sign that said; Welcome One and All to the Caring Recovery Center Where our goal is to provide Hope, Courage and Strength in Recovery. The building was a beautiful light beige with white alternating brick. There were no windows and the front doors had black tinting. The parking lot had about three other cars besides mine. I open the trunk and we unload all Aunt Debs belongings. I look at her with a warm comforting smile, she could see how proud I was of her. "Well Aunt Deb, are you ready?" With a nervous, shaky voice she said, "Well as ready as I will ever be." I grab some bags out of the trunk and we proceed to walk up to the black tinted front doors. They are locked. Next to the door is a speaker with a black button and a note that says push for buzzer. I pushed the buzzer. A Mousey voice comes over the speaker, " Go around the side please." "Um, But I am Brittney Owens and I am here to bring my Aunt Debbie Owens, we enrolled her into your program a couple of days ago." "Please go around the side *OF THE* building, Thank you!" I look at Aunt Deb, "Ok, weird."

We proceeded to go around the side of the building. We walked down the walk way, along the walk were beautiful tulips and pansies planted. All different vibrant colors. Aunt Deb grabs my attention pointing ahead. It was beautiful, nothing I ever saw before. Gardens of beautiful flowers, all types and colors and brick walk ways; every other brick had a name with two dates on them . The hedges were cut into figures and animals, wow I though. How peaceful and tranquil this could be. We see a hand full of workers pulling weeds and mulching. Hmm, I thought to myself, only three cars? Does the staff carpool? My daze was distracted by the warmth tone and welcoming voice of a woman.

"Hello! You must be Debbie." My Aunt doesn't talk just nods and smiles. "Well Debbie, my name is Jessica but you may call me Jess. I am the Chief Resident Advisor. I will be your Resident advisor. Do you have any nicknames you would like everyone to call you by?" She bats her eyes and looks at her smiling as she take some bags from me. Nervously Aunt Deb stumbles out her words "Deb will do." I speak up, "Jess this place is absolutely gorgeous. Your staff keeps it well managed." "Oh Hun that's not staff. They're residents. You see here at the Caring Center we believe that our resident need structure in their everyday lives. Not only do we help them with their journey to recovery, but we also prepare them to be self-sufficient outside of the Caring Center." I think to myself, wow what a wonderful place! This is just what Aunt Deb needs.

****

For the first two weeks Aunt Deb wasn't allowed any phone calls or any visitation until they were completely detoxified; that depended on what the doctor thought, it could be longer but on average two weeks. After two weeks we received a phone call it was for dad. He was the second, and proud to be that person, that Aunt Deb called. She was inviting him up for family day. She had completed Step one in the caring program. Step two was participation in family events, family and friend visits and three phone calls every other day. They were having a party, BBQ and karaoke for the families. Dad sadly declined as he had a three day certification course to build up more credit towards his Master auto-technician certificate and learn how to work On Dodge's new release of the Viper. He was going to be the only auto- technician in the Northern eastern area that knows and is certified to work on a Dodge Viper. I told him to tell her I will be there with the boys. I hear the cheering through the receiver of the phone. When the conversation finished dad smiled and said Thank you.

We arrived at the Caring center for family day. I was frustrated at Kevin constantly complaining about the long ride and his chanting of *"ARE WE THERE YET?"* Over and Over again. Not to mention Corey at the time was only a year and a half and hated car rides, so I had to endure screaming and crying the whole forty-five minute ride. I was relieved to arrive. The parking lot had few cars which made me to think that not many families were very supportive. Kevin flew out of the car as I got the stroller out and opened to put Corey in. We went down the walk way and see everyone laughing and joking around; having a wonderful time. Aunt Deb stops pacing as she caught a glimpse of us walking down the sidewalk. She comes dashing down almost stumbling, smiling with open arms. Kevin runs and jumps into her arms. I knew it made her happy as she wiped a tear from her face. The afternoon was beautiful, the sun shone bright in the ocean blue sky. Everyone was having a great time. Aunt Deb introduced us to her group leader, roommate and friends; all whom were very nice and polite people. Not at all like the people Aunt Deb used to hang out. We got a tour of the building and even got to sit in on an open AA Meeting which was interesting; my interest was disturbed by a very unhappy two year old, Corey. Aunt Deb played with the boys and chased them around the gardens as I watched and smiled while they laughed and giggled. I looked at my Aunt differently, she seemed different; more mature. I was proud.

I made sure I visited Aunt Deb twice a week; I really enjoyed my visits with her. We talked and talked. She talked about what she wanted to do when she got out of the caring center. They were going to help her get into a training program to work in nursing or rehab facilities.

After a year and a half, Aunt Deb had finally completed the program. I showed up for her going away party. She was leaving the Caring center. After much hugs, tears and tissues flying all about we walked down that same walk we did a year and a half ago…..

Chapter Seven:

My closest Aunt succumbs to Addiction

I was always with my Aunt Jean growing up, ever since she had her first child and especially after her second. She had decided to go back to school to finish her accountant degree. I agreed to be her babysitter, so she may accomplish her dreams. I was so proud of her; the thought never bothered me about being her constant babysitter. Everyone said I was special, that I had the patience of a Saint when it came to babies, toddlers and children. They were right I absolutely *LOVED* babies and children. I had so much fun playing with them; it was the best thing in the world to see the smiles on their faces.

Aunt Jean would leave every morning at seven am and come home between six and seven pm; just in time for bath and bedtime routine. Those girls grew an attachment to me and I them. It was hard when Aunt Jean had finally graduated with her degree.

****

It seemed around the time of my wedding back in 2003 that she started to drink more than her usual one glass of wine. I didn't think anything about it; after all it was a celebration! From there I noticed she started to drink wine while cooking dinner, at dinner, after and before bed. It wasn't only one glass each time; it was two at times three and/or four.

One evening, Aunt Jean and I were driving around looking for an open liquor store. It was this evening I noticed that she had a serious problem. We went into this small liquor store and she approaches the gentleman at the counter. Not one to be nosey I started down the nearest Isle and pretended I was looking at the bottles. She joins me moments later.

"Do you see anything you want?"

I cleared my throat, "No thank you Aunt Jean but you know I don't drink."

Aunt Jean's face turned from her natural shade, to pink then rosy red, mumbling sorry under her breath. Out comes the gentleman carrying two medium sized boxes. He brings them out to the car and puts one on one side of the other. Hearing the clanking of glass my mind begins to wonder….

"Aunt Jean, You plan on having a party or something? That's quite a lot of liquor."

Silence fills the space in the car; I'm looking at my Aunt for an answer as she stares at the road so intensely. Either she is ignoring me or she is in a deep day dream. It is silent the rest of the way to her house.

We had arrived at her house and she took two bottles of Boons Farm White Zinfandel out and placed them into the fridge. She then proceeds to go down two the basement with the remainder of the two boxes. I was dumb founded. It was then that my Aunt Jean had acquired a serious issue with drinking. This was not like her; something else was going on, deep down inside. I just had a sickening gut feeling.

It wasn't until one Christmas eve that we all found out the truth of what why Aunt Jean hid behind the Alcohol. No one except Grandma O knew of what Aunt Jean was going through and knew of her speaking to

Kim for quite some time now. Aunt Jean already has been drinking her Boone's Farm wine and was drunken by now. I don't exactly recall how or why it happened but out came those dreaded words that made the room so silent, you could hear a pin drop in a haystack. She screamed that Kelly's accusations were right about my dad, because he had molested her when she was eight or nine. Mouth's dropped open, eyes widened. I thought my Uncle was going to kill my father.

My grandmother steps in and tells us all to calm down and now isn't the time to talk about it. Aunt Jean screamed at her and blamed her for hiding it all these years, she knew everything. We all looked at each other confused; we didn't know whether to cry or to be furious. This was no place for any of us children to be around for this kind of conversation. But Aunt Jean didn't care, she blurted out how her brother bribed her with toys he would get her if he allowed her to do things and vice-versa. Needless to say after arguing and almost an all out brawl, Aunt Jean grabbed her coat and her family and walked out the door. She never talked to my father again. I was in dismay; In my mind I started doubting things. *If this happened to Kelly and Aunt Jean, could it be possible… could it? Have happened to me? Just like Josie said maybe from all the tragedy I went through my childhood could it have been so tragic I pushed it so far down I repressed the memories to protect myself??*

Things took for the worst when she began to play this online game and started talking to this guy out in California. Weeks, then months passed by; Aunt Jean became obsessed with this game and felt she fell in love with this man. When her and my Uncle Todd separated she had nowhere to go, everyone denied having her live with them. I couldn't leave her with nowhere to go, I needed to help her and I will lay down the law. I told her, "Absolutely *NO* alcohol in my house! We don't drink and we have two young children. I expect you to clean up after yourself. If you can follow those two rules then my house is your house."

She smiled as a tear rolled down her face. "I'm so proud of you! You have truly grown to be a beautiful and strong young woman." She pulled me toward her and hugged me so tight it felt like I was going to pass out. "I love you too Aunt Jean."

Two weeks went by and everything was going great. Aunt Jean had even asked me to bring her to some AAA meetings each week. I felt like I had done some good for my Aunt and it's true that there is hope for everyone. Of course every day I had to put up with fights from my parents and the rest of the family for having Aunt Jean live with me. My parents most of all, they felt that she wasn't recovering and that I was blind to it. They reminded me of how I was little and at every holiday we kids always thought it was funny that Aunt Deb (one of my father's three sisters') always hid her vodka bottles. They told me to open my eyes and look all around inside and outside of the house for empty bottles.

The very next day I was cleaning my boys room and vacuuming when I heard clang, clang under the bed; the vacuum had hit something, something glass? I crawled under the bed as far as I could, with my arms reached out to its fullest, my finger tips just barely touching the tip feeling the glass. I get out from under the bed and pull the bunk beds out from behind the wall and to my surprise I find not one, not two but three empty wine bottles. I was furious; I went into mamma bear mode. She is drinking wine as she reads my *BABIES* bed time stories! I tried; I thought I could help her. I revert back to Step One of the twelve steps of Al-Anon; *"We admitted we were powerless over alcohol—that our lives had become unmanageable."*)* You can only make progress when you know and practice the first step.

I see and understand this step as Enabling and asking for strength from your higher power to let go of what you cannot change. There is an excerpt I go back in my Al-Anon book whenever I feel that I may or seem to become powerless over anything in my life; it helps me gain control of myself and my life again.

"I pray to be released from my compulsion to control my situation. I have so often proved I am unable to control it. Let me think, know and feel my powerfulessness; then I will at least learn to let go and let God.")*

If only I had known what I know now, then. I was an enabler in every way. I did not want to kick her out. I am too kind hearted; besides she is my Aunt. I respect her. My parents decided without discussing with me to come to my house and kick her out. This made me mad. What right did they have? What right did they have to kick any guest out of my house I choose to stay here? Control. This I have come to know and understand about my family at an early age. *CONTROL*, everyone had to have control. There were too many chiefs and no Indians. No wonder they always butted heads.

My Aunt decided to move in with Uncle Jim and Aunt Paige out in Sanderson, Ca. We were blind to the fact that the guy she had been talking to online conveniently lived twenty minutes away. It didn't take long for Uncle Jim and Aunt Paige to kick her out. They kept everything a secret from the whole family except for Grandma O, but she didn't tell a single soul. This enraged my Uncle Todd (Aunt Jean's husband), and her two Children Serenity and Carley. They were kept in the dark regarding their mom.

Aunt Jean drank from morning until bed. She was drunk all the time and over taking her anxiety pills. She moved in with this man she met online She loved so much. She had only lived out in California for one and one-half year before she drank so much and took all the pills that ended her life.

June 25, 2009

As I sit back reflecting on my life; living with this so called disease "*addiction*" and how it has affected my life in so many ways good and bad, I think...... What is *addiction*? Experts characterize it as *"an excessive consumption of and dependence on their drug of choice and or alcoholic beverages leading to physical, psychological harm and social and vocational functioning."*)* So they say… But I have seen it and experienced it in very different ways. I have seen it as a silent, deadly killer that consumes its victims and eats away at them from the inside out until there is nothing left, not even a soul….

I look to the sky, watching the dark clouds shield the beaming sun. There is a battle going on as the sun fights to peek through the thick murkiness of the clouds….. Sorrow fills the air. My mind begins to wander back to that dreaded phone call moments ago…. Words I thought I'd never thought or wanted to hear. I just lost my Aunt. A beautiful soul both inside and out who fell prey to the horrible disease of Alcoholism. Tears fill my eyes as I drive down the road, my four year old singing along with the music in the back seat, not knowing what's going on. I can't help myself but to think of all the wonderful and beautiful memories I have of her. I can't help myself to cry even harder thinking how my boys will never know how beautiful, how wonderful she was. How vibrant and alive she was, the way she walked into the room and had everyone's attention. She made sure of that! She was the life of the party.

Corey, who is four years old at the time, quickly diverts my attention to him. Sounding annoyed he asked me if we were there yet. I grumble annoyed as this is his 5th time in the past five minutes he has asked me. I assure him I will let him know as soon as we get there. Corey is my special boy. He is autistic, I've know he has been since the time he was 6 months old. Doctor after doctor has told me no he is not on the spectrum. I have had to be his advocate and fight for him until he was finally diagnosed at six years old. Anxiousness and repetition are just one of the many qualities he possesses as an autistic child. We are on our way to pick up my son Kevin from Soccer camp. I answered Corey quickly and turned my attention back to day dreaming reflecting back on my childhood.

I begin to say the Serenity prayer over and over in my head. It's a prayer that I live by day to day. I look to the sky as a smile comes across my face, I chuckle. The sun shines bright, the grey clouds have retreated…. Victory is in the air! My thoughts fill with wonder and gratefulness that after thirty-one years I have had the Strength and Courage not to take a sip and let the drink consume my inner soul…. These are my memoirs of an alcoholic family, only it felt normal…

It was never easy growing up with an Alcoholic and drug addicted father. As a matter of fact my father and his siblings either are alcoholics', drug addicts or have tendencies to become addicts. Experts say *"Alcoholism has evidence that it has a genetic component")**, and that may be so. But my opinion and throughout my life my experience with Alcoholism and addiction; I learned that it is a learned behavior and a choice. You can choose to follow what you see growing up or you can choose to learn from your parents' or families' experiences and mistakes. I have learned much from Al-Anon and Al-Ateen.

One excerpt I learned that sticks out in my head is: *"I can live my life only one day at a time. Perhaps my confusion and despair are so great that I will have to take it one hour at a time, or one minute at a time, reminding myself constantly that I have the authority over no life but my own. Realizing that nothing can hurt me while I lean upon my higher power, I ask to be guided through the hours and minutes of each day. Let me remind myself to bring to myself every problem to Him for I know He will show me the way I must go.")**

I arrive at Soccer camp and a very excited Kevin jumps into the car. He straightens up and says proudly "I made three goals today!" I fight to hold back a tear and put on an excited face, "Awesome job!!!!! Mommy is <u>SO PROUD</u> of you!!!" Deep down my heart was breaking. How could I ruin his special day with such bad news of Aunt Jiji? Aunt Jiji is what all her Great Niece and nephews called her.

We arrive home; automatically I start to cook dinner. We're having an early dinner tonight as I want to go and be there for my two cousins. They are fourteen and seventeen and just lost their mother. In the background I hear Kevin calling for me asking me what Aunt Jiji's phone number was as he wanted to tell her the good news. When my Aunt lived with us she always played soccer and helped Kevin out with the sport. My eyes swelled and tears just poured down my face. I wiped the tears from my face as I sat him down and tell him that Aunt Jiji is in Heaven now that she is there with Pop. Pop is my grandfather and Kevin's Great grandfather. He always called him Pop. Kevin understood that he would never see Aunt Jiji again. He loved Aunt Jiji so I had to make him understand that he wouldn't see her again that she was gone.

Grandma asked me to do Aunt Jean's Eulogy; I was honored to do so. She also asked me to make the slideshow disc for the viewing as I had the program. Every Great Nephew and Niece was asked to put an item into Aunt Jiji's casket so she can take a piece of them with her. Kevin put a Soccer picture of him, Josh put a baseball, Corey put a picture of her and Aunt Jiji together, and Ben put one of his favorite toys. Mass was beautiful and everyone complimented me on my Eulogy. It took everything I had to hold back the tears as I read what I wrote. It was so beautiful Grandma asked me to make her a copy of it.

It's hard to realize that my Aunt is gone; sometimes it feels just like yesterday we were just laughing and talking on the couch. No one realizes the impact suicide has on a loved one. My cousins were just fourteen and seventeen when she took her life. My Aunt will never see them get married or have children. They went through a very hard time in their life, always wondering if their mother loved them and why? Why would she leave them? Why did she do this? Was it them? They will never get the answers. They're answers no one will get a solution too.

"Although all man/woman have a common destiny, each individual also has to work out his personal salvation for him/herself.... We can help one another find out the meaning of life.... But in the last analysis, each is responsible for 'finding him/herself") **

Chapter Eight:
My Sister's Addiction and Recovery

Krystal did not like rules at all; which is why she moved out at the age of seventeen. She worked mo as her optician during the day and for the Holly diner in the evenings. As part of her pay she stayed in one of their hotel rooms behind the diner. Her and Mark lived in the one bedroom hotel room. It was quite small, with a living room and a very small, non-functional kitchenette area. She traveled thirty minutes from Holly to Medford to work.

Mom had a cute office in a little shopping plaza; it was off the main road in Medford. The building was white with black trim. Inside mom and the Dr had it remodeled. The walls were inviting, beige with a light ivy green trim. The lights shining bright on the fixtures for the glasses made them glisten. Mom's office had a much bigger optical and waiting area than her boss' office did. The business was flourishing and things couldn't be going any better.

After I had Kevin, Krystal became pregnant. She went for a routine exam and told her primary doctor, Dr. Gregory Forte that she had noticed a black spot on her inner thigh. The doctor asked her how long has it been there and Krystal shrugged her shoulders.

"Maybe a year or so, it's only gotten bigger in the past couple of months."

"Let me look and examine the mass." He takes a look at the large, black mass. He feels and squeezes it, it is hard. "Did it hurt when I did that?" He looks very concerned, Krystal's face turns pale from the melancholy look on his face.

"A little." Krystal says dubiously…

"Krystal, I would like you to go see a dermatologist and get a biopsy of that." The doctor sounded very concerned and worrisome. Krystal was confused, "Ok, is this something that I should be concerned about or is this serious?"

"Krystal I am not a dermatologist but to me that looks like melanoma."

She screams "<u>MELANOMA</u>! *What*! *How*! *Why*?" She starts crying. The doctor rubs her back trying to ease her pain. "I suggest you get in as soon as you can."

"How did your doctor appointment go?" Mom says as she shovels the remainder of her lunch in her mouth before the next patient walks in. Krystal walks to her desk staring blankly and dumbfounded as she drops her purse on her chair. Mom's face turns white knowing its not good news. Krystal mumbles out the words as tears flow from her eyes; "I have to go see a dermatologist, I have Melanoma." Mom stares blankly, he mouth gapping wide open as half her sandwich falls to the floor along with a tear. "Are they sure?" A very frustrated Krystal yells out angrily "YES! I'm sorry mom. I'm too young to have cancer; Josh is only a year old. I can't deal with this." Krystal falls to her chair feeling faint she breaks down and cries. Mom runs to her side and holds her tight, so tight Krystal muffles out the words "I can't breathe mom." "Sorry, Krys. Whatever needs to be done I will be there for you every step of the way."

****

"Well Krystal that is a huge mass and it's very black. Why have you waited so long to get it checked out?" Dr. Shoemaker said very concerned. He was highly recommended by several of mom's patients and by Krystal's primary doctor, Dr. Forte. Krystal looks up at the ceiling, lips moving but no words coming out. She thinks about when the black spot appeared. "I'm not sure but it has to be at least three maybe four years?" Dr. S looks concerned, "What! Krystal do you realize how serious this is?" Krystal nods as a tear escapes her eye and rolls down her cheek. "I need to do a biopsy just to make sure it's not malignant and I am ordering a PET scan to make sure it hasn't spread." Krystal nods her head.

"I am going to give you a shot to numb the area where the spot is. It's called Lidocaine. I want you to tell me at any time when I am cutting a piece off if you have any pain. I will give you a stronger numbing shot." Krystal nods grabbing mom's hand. "Ready?" She nods. "One, two, three! All done." "Wow that wasn't so bad." "No Krystal, that's the easy part. The hard part is yet to come."

The anticipation of waiting for the results was torture for all of us. The doctor did say it could take seven to fourteen days for the results to come in and she would call right away. Words raced through my head, my baby sister may have cancer. Just like mom did when we were babies. They say history repeats itself; NO she can't! She is too young, she has yet to live! She has a baby to take care of she doesn't need this! Why Lord, Why? Why do you throw so much turmoil, pain and suffering at us, what have we done to deserve this?!

For the first time in my life I felt vulnerable to alcohol addiction. I actually felt like having a drink, not just any drink… Shots and Beer would do. I started to walk to the nearest bar. I walked up the steps and proceeded to open the door and stopped. I shook off the thought and went to the nearest AA meeting. I shared my story, I felt it would help me as I almost had that sip and would have drowned myself in a sea of alcohol.

On the ninth day Krystal received that dreaded phone call, she did in fact test positive for malignant melanoma but luckily it hadn't spread yet.

She was lucky for that. Thank you Lord for small favors. Dr. Shoemaker made an appointment for Krystal to come into her surgery center that was attached to her office building. She was going to remove the cancer and send the specimen to Grace Savior Cancer Institute in St. Clair, NY. Grace Savior was one of the top three Cancer hospitals in the world. This is where Krystal will receive her treatments.

Krystal wasn't allowed to eat or drink anything before surgery despite the fact that she wasn't being totally knocked out only in twilight. Mom took her to Dr. S's surgery center and was allowed to be in the room with her but had to wear a sterilized gown, hair net, gloves, mask, and booties. Krystal laughed at how funny and ridiculous mom looked. At least it got her mind off the surgery. The surgery took approximately forty minutes when it should have been only about twenty minutes the most. They had some complications; Dr. Shoemaker didn't expect to have to cut into Krystal's leg so deep. The melanoma was rooted to her inner hamstring about an inch and three quarters deep and the spot was approximately seven millimeters wide. The doctor prescribed Krystal an antibiotic to prevent infection and vicodin 7.5mg/300mg. This is where her addiction started....

****

Krystal and mom arrive at Grace Savior; Krystal was to get one round of radiation and 3 months of chemotherapy; despite the fact that Dr. Shoemaker removed all the cancer. This was just being precautious. The Oncologist at GSCI gave her a prescription to help with the nausea and vomiting symptoms; he told her all follow up care would be done through Dr. Shoemaker and that the doctor would keep him informed. If anything changed or she felt something was not right she was to call his office and his secretary would get her in right away.

Over the next few months Krystal went back to her dermatologist for her follow up visit. She explained how she was still in pain, complained that she kept feeling this tingling feeling going down her right leg causing her leg to weaken and causing her to fall unexpectedly. She said all this was causing her major anxiety and she has become panicky due to the fact that she works two jobs and is a single mother supporting a two and half year old. Dr. Shoemaker ordered her a nerve and muscle test, prescribed her 120 vicodin 7.5mg/300mg 3-4 times a day as needed for pain and 120 Klonopin 1mg 3-4 tablets as needed for anxiety and panic attacks. Both of these medicines are highly addictive if misused; and that's exactly what Krystal did.... Misuse them. She had her tests and found that during her surgery one of her nerves was accidently cut which is why she got the tingling down her leg.

When Krystal ran out early she would call my Aunt; Dr. Sophia Burke. She knew everything going on with what Krystal was going through so she was more than happy to help her out. She would call in her prescriptions into Krystal's pharmacy; this was before these medicines were still allowed to be called in and no longer allowed and you had to bring the script in. This went on for a year; her doctor would call her prescriptions in every month, then mid month Aunt Sophia would call in her prescriptions. My Aunt noticed things about Krystal at family functions, she seemed different and she seemed high all the time. She took Krystal aside and made up an excuse as to why she couldn't prescribe her the vicodins and klonopins anymore. Krystal pleaded and begged her all the while crying.

"I can't sleep Aunt Sophia." She sniffled and cried. "The pain keeps me awake and I begin to panic. I can't handle it all, I am falling apart."

"I am sorry Krystal, but when it comes down to losing my license I have to do what's best for me." She was sympathetic, caring and loving; pulling Krystal into her arms and consoling her.

I never mentioned one very important thing about my little sister Krystal. She was a drama queen and a *VERY GOOD* actress. She could convince anyone anything. If she said the sky was red, she would come up with this unbelievable reason that was so unbelievable that it was believable and you really thought the sky was red. Our family always joked around saying if Krystal was a real actress she would win an Academy Award! But Krystal couldn't pull the wool over my Aunt's eyes. You see my Aunt is a very smart person, she graduated Valedictorian both in high school and in college. She had called Krystal's dermatologist and spoke with her about the prescriptions she had prescribed her. She found out that Dr. Shoemaker had taken her off the medicines six months ago and suggested that she see a pain management specialist for the pain and her primary doctor for her anxiety, as she was only allowed to prescribe those medicines for a brief period of time. It was then that my Aunt knew Krystal had a problem and was addicted to her pain medicine and the Klonopin.

Krystal had no choice but to go see our family doctor, Dr. Gregory Forte. Dr. Forte's office was in Medford, right down the road from mom's office. He would make it a top priority to take anyone of us in at any time; all five of us had been seeing him as our family doctor ever since we moved up to Pennsylvania seventeen years ago. We had been one of his few beginning patients; he'd just expanded his practice in Medford, PA and had his other practice in Newtown, NJ. Krystal explained everything to Dr. Forte in her usual dramatic way, topping the cake off with a cherry by breaking down and crying lavishly. He prescribed her the same medicines as Dr. Shoemaker had except he gave her 240 tablets of Vicodin 10mg/300mg for a thirty day supply and he increased her Klonopin from 1mg to 2mg 120 tablets 3-4 tablets as needed. As if what Dr. Shoemaker gave her wasn't enough?!

Months passed, then another year gone. Krystal got her prescriptions from Dr. Forte every month, sometime a week or two early, going to different pharmacy's she hadn't gone to so they couldn't see that she ran out of meds too soon; she always paid for her meds in cash. It wasn't until 2005 when the family noticed something different about Krystal; Kim and I were the first to notice. Krystal had stopped attending family functions, she stopped answering calls, during summers she would ask me if Josh could stay with me for a week as he and Keith were close and I lived in a community with a pool inside and outside. She would drop him off on a Sunday with a couple boxes of Mac and cheese, a box of cereal and two boxes of fruit snacks. She gave me money for bread and milk for the week. The week came and went, two weeks went by and no word from Krystal. I called her to see what was going on; not that I minded Josh staying with us, I enjoyed having him there. He kept Keith company and off my case so I could concentrate on Corey (whom was an infant at the time). The boys got along well and we had wonderful summers together. Krystal never answered her calls when I called; I of course being mother hen started to panic and become distressed. She never even called to check up on him or to talk to him. I remember the time when mom and dad told us how dad's sister Aunt Dana would do the same thing with our cousin Jake when he was a baby. Jake and I were a year apart; my parents knew Aunt Dana had an alcohol and drug addiction and talked about adopting Jake as she did this quite often.

Kim and I talked about Krystal and her "*random and irregular*" behaviors often. We knew she was into more than her pills. We both decided to converse with mom and dad about our apprehension and regards to Krystal's atypical behaviors. We had already spoken to dad about wanting to speak with Krystal and asked him to call her and get her to come over. On the way to mom and dad's house Kim and I discussed how we could break the news delicately to mom, we knew dad wouldn't be a problem. We've had mini conversations with him about Krystal and he has agreed with us but can't put his finger on what drug she is on. We arrived at our parents' house, our childhood home we grew up in. It was so different since the time we first moved in; dad and I did a lot of remodeling inside and out.

Kim gets out of the car, I sit behind the wheel gripping the steering wheel so tight my knuckles turn the shade of white, my face pale, butterflies flutter in my stomach, I feel sick, my intestines tied in knots; my IBS is kicking in. This happens when I am stressed out or nervous; I *HATE* confrontations! Kim looks at me perplexed as I heave the front car door open and slam it shut. I shriek, "IBS kicking in!" As I run towards the front door up the stairs not paying attention to what she said. I pry the screen door open so fast and open the front door running around the hall and straight to the bathroom. Mom and dad looked discombobulated as Kim walked in saying "IBS." Both mom and dad said in harmony "Ooooh." Kim blurts out " You know how Mel is, She hates confrontation and get all sick over it." In consensus mom and dad intone declare, "Yep, we know her all too well."

I walk into the living room and no sooner do I sit in walks Krystal. She is wearing a sweat shirt, its bulky and immense on her; it just evidently doesn't fit at all. What is this? In the middle of the summer heat, this was clue # one. Clue # two was that she looked like skin and bones and had dark bags under her eyes. She looked doped out and looked like a crack head.

"Holy Crap Krys, you look like shit where did you go? Though we lost you under all those slovenly botched and disheveled clothing? There goes Kim's unfiltered mouth again… I glance over and give her the evil eye. She brushes it off.

Krystal was antagonized and responded in a pompous way "Well, Gee Kim thanks for the vote of confidence and it's good to see you to. You look quite overabundance yourself, oh and loudmouthed as always." She taunted Kim with a scorned grin. As Krystal passed Kim went to lunge at her as I put myself between the two; I knew it couldn't be a good thing; Kim would crush her and just because she was a big person but because she got psychotic quick and you best watch out. I was the only one who could calm her down and could kick her ass if needed and she knew that; thou she was much bigger than I. She walked over to the couch and sat down by mom and said Hi to her and dad then started a conversation with mom.

"Ah hem." Dad interrupted. His voice was soft, concerned and he was to the point. We all knew he meant business. All eyes turned to him. I was glad he was the conversation starter but hoped and crossed my fingers he didn't ask my opinion on these circumstances.

"We didn't have you girls over for a fun family get together. I would like complete honesty from all three of you girls." There is a 2 minute pause. I look at mom; she turns her head away from Krystal towards dad as tears rolls down her face. She then looks at me and Kim who are sitting across the room on the other couch. Butterflies rippled through my stomach fast and faster; oh Lord I'm going to vomit. I can feel and see mom's pain, Krystal of course was the baby; her baby. Mom was in complete denial. Does she not remember what she has learned, what she was taught in Al- Anon?? What has she been doing? Sleeping? Mo has a tendency to fall asleep very easily; she has been diagnosed with narcolepsy. Has she been doing her step work?? This is *EXACTLY* what step seven is all about. Apparently she hasn't done her step work or fell asleep the day step seven was talked about. Step seven: *"Humbly asked him to remove all our short comings."** What this step is telling us is that we need to be ready to remove all our shortcomings which include your denial in the addict. We Need to *"humbly"* ask God/your higher power for help to remove these shortcomings, but not all at once. You take one at a time as not to overwhelm yourself. One at a time, One day at a time. It means you won't be alone to remove these shortcomings; your higher power will be there to help and guide you.

My fist ascent ready to throw a punch. "Oww!!" I yelped coming back to reality. Kim had pinched my arm. I gave her a look and she knew what that meant; slowly sliding down the couch trying to scoot as fast as she could I grabbed the loop of her jeans and pulled her to me and my fist came down on her thigh like fists of war. "WTF. What was that for?" Kim rubbing her leg "You were inattentive and we've beckoned you several times…" "Oh I am sorry I was observing in deep profound thought."

An embittered Kim explain in brief detail what conversation has been going on and that mom was in complete denial and on Krys' side. I looked at Mo and flashed her a look as if looks could kill. I spoke to her fiercely and never had done that before but needed to put my foot down. She needed to know what she was doing was wrong and she *HAD* to go back to Al-Anon and start all over again.

"Mo, when did you stop going to Al-Anon?"

"Maybe a year and half ago? Not quite sure?" I looked at her in frustration, "Have you ever worked on step Seven?" Krystal folds her arms in anger, "What has this got to do with any of this?"

"Look at you Krystal, just take a moral inventory of yourself! You have changed drastically since you have moved out. You've lost so much weight that your skin and bones and the only way I know that you can do that is by using cocaine.

You don't call any of us; you don't attend family events, and just look at you what are you doing wearing a sweater in eight-nine degree weather?? Plus your face looks like you're on some hard-core drugs!"

"Brittney Ann!!" Mom was furious.

I looked at her from across the room with a scowl. "How dare you mo. Did we not tell you, especially dad that you are allowed to listen but not open your mouth? You are in denial and are biased. Krystal cannot do any wrong in your eyes. Let me ask you something Mo? What did you learn in Al-Anon, or did you sleep through the denial and step seven class?"

"Al-Anon is anonymity and I don't have to tell you anything." She replied snooty with arms folded.

"Oh, so we're playing that game are we?" I looked Mom straight in the eyes, they were burning with fire. "Well then *LET ME REFRESH* your memory. *"Step Seven: Humbly asked him to remove our shortcomings.")* Do you remember that step? Did you *REALLY* work on it with your sponsor?" I didn't even give mo a chance to answer; by this time Krystal was pissed; her only ally was being attacked. "I don't think you have. If you did then you wouldn't be *ENABLING* Krystal!" My voice got loud and you could hear the fury and frustration in my words. Mom sat there speechless as did, Kim and dad staring at me with gapping mouths open. I've never been so outspoken before or said my peace. They knew this hit *TOO* close to home for me.

"Mo, I have watched you make one excuse after another and another for Krystal. You know that is called enabling. I've seen you give her money as she cried poverty, even thou she makes plenty of money on the two jobs she has. You have given her the business card as she cried that she can't do it all as a single mother and that Josh needs clothing and formula." I laughed. "Well were was money for Kim and I when we struggled with our babies? We never went on a shopping spree on your business! Mo tried to get a word in as I cut her off with a gesture of my finger across my neck. I watch as Krystal glares at me, arms folded. She is furious now as her legs begin to anxiously bounce. "Listen Mo, I am not attacking you, I am just merely showing you how you are enabling her. I know your intentions are good, kind and some can be uncontrollable. It's an impulsive action to try and try to help Krystal see the light. But in doing so you are creating a monster!"

Krystal stands up and stomps out of the living room, "I don't have to hear any of this. This is so unfair, you're all attacking me except mom." I chuckle, "No one is attacking you Krys, first of all it's been me talking, and you haven't heard Kim or dad yet." She stomps out through the kitchen and towards the door. Dad turn to her, "Krystal Marie you sit your ass down now. We're not done!" Krys starts to cry and slowly walks back to the couch by mom. "How dare you get up and leave in the middle of our conversation! And do not give me your acting tactics, I'm not in the mood to see you get an academy award. I *DON'T* hand them out!"

You could see Krystal's eyes swell up, they turn red and puffy. "Well everyone is attacking me and Britt is screaming at me and making me seem like I'm some kind of monster!" "Krystal I apologize for that. I wasn't screaming at you, you are taking my concerns and actions as attacking you and screaming at you when in fact; my intentions were never meant to hurt you, I, we only want to help you before this goes any further. The way your acting is exactly what we have learned in Al-Ateen. Don't you remember? You are in complete denial."

"For the millionth time people I am not on drugs!!! So stop with your pathetic interventions. I've had enough but I'm sorry I need get ready to go to work at the Honky Tonk. She speed walks out of the door before any one could say anything.

I look at mom she is crying, "Great now she will never come around!"

"Mom, I hate to say this to you and maybe it's not my place to say it and maybe it is. But you do need to realize that you are enabling her."

"I am not! Now your attacking me Britt? What is going on here? Where losing our family."

"Do you remember what you learned in Al-Anon? Let me refresh your memory with an excerpt from the book." I take out the book One Day At A Time In Al-Anon from my purse; I carry this around like it's my bible. I proceed to turn to page 308 and read the excerpt to mom.

"*Detachment motivated by love can shield us from needless pain and set the stage for a truly rewarding relationship.*")* "Do you understand that mo?"

"*NO*!" She cries, wiping tears from her eyes, giving me the evil eye.

"I know you blame me, but this needed to be done for the both of you. Regardless of what you say, you really are in denial. I believe you do need to go back to Al-Anon. This statement reminds us that we certainly are concerned about our loved one or people in our lives who maybe an alcoholic like dad, or a drug addict like Krystal. The detachment is for your protection so you don't get drawn into her/his turmoil and crisis that she/he is creating. You think you can help her when in fact she doesn't want to be helped. This detachment is a healthy Al-Anon way of preventing you from hurting you and hopefully her not taking advantage of you as she has been. Mo, I really would like you to go back, I have attend myself due to Krystal's addiction for help to understand her. I have also attended open NA meetings to see what the drug addict experiences and how they struggle day after day but stay sober for whatever reason. What do you think Mo, you want to join me? I go on my lunch and you can practically walk to the meeting. I'll be there for you and help guide you."

"Ok, Britt, I will go with you." It seemed as thou she forced the words out of her mouth. She got up and went to her bedroom closing the door behind her. Kim and dad stand up the look of astonishment on their face for my encouraging words, I can tell they were proud of the person I had become. Kim hugged me and smiled, dad walked over me put his hands on my shoulders and pulled me in and held me tight. He whispered in my ear, "I am so proud of the woman you have become, thank you."

****

Josh was about three years old when his immature and childish father, Mark took him on the four-wheeler on Lake Silver Holy. The lake was beautiful in the spring and summertime. It was rich with all varieties of fish and was a huge fishing spot. The lake was surrounded by the most beautiful houses as well as boat launches. All houses had their own docks and the marina was on the west side, south east of the beach. Lake Silver Holy was the biggest lake in the area with a length of 13.05 miles long and an area of 8,906 miles. It is the third largest manmade lake in Pennsylvania. In the winter it was crowded with fishermen ice fishing hoping to get that big prize fish everyone wanted. No ATV's riding around the iced up lake were allowed as the power company who owned the Lake prohibited it. Some parts of the lake especially the middle weren't fully frozen. Mark wasn't the brightest bulb in the box. He did stupid things that he thought was so funny; he burnt every brain cell he had on drugs and alcohol. On this particular day, Krystal thought Mark was taking Josh ice fishing; instead he had this great idea of driving his four-wheeler across Lake Silver Holly with his three year old son. Well I am sure you guessed what happened next and your right. Mark was doing figure eights in the middle of the lake as Josh scream "Yay!! Faster!" Not knowing what danger lies ahead. Mark went faster and decided to go out further; he needed a longer stretch to get the four-wheeler up to speed. He slammed hard on his break when he heard the ice start to crack. He spun around as fast as he could but it was too slushy and his tires got stuck. The back end started to sink and before you knew it the four-wheeler, Josh and Mark went through the ice. They were ok, but the four-wheeler sunk to the bottom of the lake. When Krystal found this out that was the beginning of the end of their decade long relationship. She felt he was more of a child than an adult and acted as such whenever he had Josh. She couldn't trust him to be alone with Josh; it scared her.

Krystal continued to work her two jobs, she had quit the dinner and kept working at the optical and the bar/restaurant. She lived very comfortably as a single mom, never asking Josh for a single penny. Aunt Jean had started doing the books for mom all the while becoming the manager of the new vision therapy office in Medford. She taught me how to do the books and file for quarterly taxes for the business and I was working part time as her vision therapist and full time at Wal-Mart as the Head Customer Service Manager. I had always had an impeccable work ethic, I was what you would call a workaholic. I would immerse myself in my work to forget the tragedy I had been through. I guess that was my downfall besides smoking pot.

I was never the type of person to talk about what happened to me or what my problems were and ask for help to find solutions to them. I always held them inside and pushed them down so deep no one would ever know; besides being humiliated, mortified, at blame I didn't want anyone else to feel the same way about me. That wasn't the person who I was. I was always there for my family, running to their every needs and helping them anyway I could. I put them before myself all my life; especially my mom. I could never say no to her, it was like she had me wrapped around her little finger. She had a rough life, I knew this. She taught me how to be like her; a strong, personable woman. She was the poster woman of strength, compassion and positivity; her attitude bestowed upon me. Everyone in the family always told me that out of all three of us girls I was the most like my mom and for that I was so proud holding my head up high feeling privileged and dignified.

While Krystal worked at The Honkey Tonk friends would drop Josh off after pre-school until the end of her shift if it wasn't a late shift. If she worked late she had a babysitter which they would come for diner and then go to Krys' house afterwards. The Honkey Tonk was a Bar/Restaurant/Hotel; the parking lot was very small only fitting maybe ten cars in the lot. Across from the bar was a bank where people would park when it would get busy. As you walked into the bar the hallway was filled with smoke and drunken people stumbling up the stairs to their rooms or to the bathrooms to the left of me. Getting into the door was always jammed packed. The music was bellowed throughout the bar as the beat of the music resonated while people danced between the bar and tables. People laughed, played pool, and shared some spirits, memories and good times with friends and family. There was always a exceptional inclination in the atmosphere. As you walked into the bar was to your left, it was a beautifully polished mahogany wooden bar, with sparkling glasses above that shimmered in the bars' lighting. It was eye catching; you couldn't help but to notice it when you first walked through the door. To the right of me were five booths with tables to match the bar and seat of deep burgundy. The place was absolutely beautiful and quite a sight to see. No wonder it was always busy all the time. As you walked further into the room straight ahead was the pool table. This table was top notch, a real completion table and yes they did have pool tournaments. To the left of the pool table were beautiful matching tables and booths for sit down diners; there were about 18 all together. The whole staff was very inviting, polite and always conversed with their customers. From Thursday through Sunday The Honkey Tonk had some type of entertainment, whether it be Karaoke, live music, a comedian, family night, etc... This is where she met Kyle; her future fiancé. Kyle was a Cop for the Mt. Vernon Regional Police in Pompe, PA. Krystal and Kyle became friends quickly and why wouldn't they Krystal had a bubbly, humorous personality. After knowing each other for a year they started dating. We were all relieved she had finally found a decent man that could keep her on the path of the straight and narrow. After dating for nine months she finally introduced Josh to Kyle; it was an instant attraction for both of them. Kyle and Josh took to each other like father and son. We finally met Kyle after she introduced Josh to him; we instantly liked him. He was a gentleman, very well mannered and straight to the point. He was about 6'1", with blue eyes and brown short hair. He was adorable. I remember him in school. I went to high school with him; he was two years ahead of me but his sister Judy was in my grade.

Two to three years into their relationship Kyle proposed to Krys. It was a big shock to us all as we knew Krys was NOT the committing type. She enjoyed her freedom, she enjoyed not being told what to do and to be able to come and go whenever she pleased. We all thought she would be an old maid for the rest of her life. Kyle had become a part of our family right from the beginning; we all enjoyed having him around and loved him from the start.

Kyle and Josh grew close as the years passed. Kyle showing Josh how to play baseball like he did growing up, he also showed him how to hunt. These things helped their relationship's bond to grow stronger than ever. Josh thought of Kyle as his dad and became very resentful that his real father Mark had left him to move to Florida when he was three and a half. In time that was soon forgotten and he didn't care for Mark; his real father was Kyle and still to this day is; though Kyle and his mom are no longer together. After four years they moved into Kyle's house and for the first time Josh has some stability in his life. Krystal had a habit of moving from house to house, she never stayed in one place for long.

****

Time passed, Krystal had changed... Not for the good, but for the worse. She went into hiding. She stopped coming to family functions making excuses as to why she couldn't come at first; then she wouldn't answer our calls at all. Kim and I knew that she was hooked on her pain pills again. She kept getting prescriptions from her doctor and when her doctor told her to go to pain management for the nerve damage in her leg from the cancer surgery she didn't take the doctor's advice. Instead she would call my Aunt Sophia and cry to her that she was in pain and it was causing her anxiety and panic attacks. Aunt Sophia would prescribe her, her pain pills and Klonopins. Month after month she would call our Aunt, until one day when Krys asked for an increase, my Aunt caught on and knew she was becoming addicted; she cut her off. This left Krystal with no choice but to find what she needed on the streets. She did have a choice but like so many others she choose the wrong choice; she took that deep, dark path and danced with the devil. When the pills weren't enough she started snorting them and that led her to Cocaine and when that wasn't good enough she started shooting Cocaine into her arms.

When we did see Krystal many weeks after she was hooked on Cocaine we knew immediately. She didn't look like our beautiful sister/daughter. Her eyes were sunken and blackened. Her face was thinned and you could see her bones protruding from her face down throughout her neck and shoulders. She was skinny as a rail; she had become a size zero and fit into a size 12 juniors. No way could she have dropped so much weight in such a little amount of time. Her excuse; she had been using that P32X weight lose system. But we knew better. The first clue we knew when she was shooting up was that she wore sweat shirts in the summer time. She was hiding it so we couldn't see the track marks. But she always came up with some crazy excuse that was so unbelievably believable! This time it was "Since I lost all that weight I'm always cold!" Duh, like jackasses we fell prey to her trap.

We never really would have expected Krystal to go as far as to "shoot up." Well for one she hated needles and getting her blood drawn. Two she always called people who "used needles scum bags and trash!" Three she wouldn't be able to take a needle a put it in her vein herself, she would be scared to death that she would do something horrifically and deadly wrong and it would kill her. Boy did she pull the wool over our eyes! But Kim and my guts still were twisting and turning and taking us for a loop; we knew something was not right.

One day all four of us women, my mom, two sisters and I got together and decided to have a women's night were we do fun things. I remember the laughs we had that night, besides the fact Kim and I could tell Krystal was coming down off of whatever it was that she had done. We had so many laughs sitting down telling our most memorable, funniest stories we had throughout the years. Then we convinced mo to let us straighten her hair like we had done ours, so we could take a picture of the four of us with straight hair. Mom had light brown and very curly hair. Instead of brushing her hair she would pick it or just spray it while it was wet and scrunch it with her hands. We finished mo's hair and started laughing. She looked ridiculous; definitely not a straight hair woman. Now I know why she was given curly hair. Mo ran to the mirror to see what we were laughing about.

"*EWW*! Get rid of it, take it back!"

"We can't Mo; you have to wash it to get your curl back. But first we need to take that picture." I say choking the words out as I try not to laugh.

"Gross *NOOO*! I don't want anyone to see me like this."

After swearing to God and promising we would never show anyone the picture she agreed to take the picture.

Mo was the first one to go to bed that night. Krystal excused herself; she had to go to the bathroom. We were pretty sure we knew what she was going to do. We heard the door shut and mission possible went into action. You see through the day and evening, every chance we could get we would talk about what we were going to do. We expected Krystal to either nod off as usual or tie up the bathroom for forty-five minutes. We threw our jackets on and jumped over the recliners closest to the door and out we ran. We flung open her car door and started searching it with a fine tooth comb. Until we came across the evidence we had dreaded to find…. We found the tourniquet, the needle with some blood still lingering in there and little paper bags. Kim put on the gloves on we confiscated earlier and put the evidence in a Ziploc bag we had gotten as well. We waited until morning to confront Krystal.

It was six am when dad came out of his bedroom and Kim and I woke right up. I don't know if it was my adrenaline or anxiety that got my heart pumping so fast. We quietly walked out of the living room as not to wake Krys. The Ziploc bag we had put in a brown bag so Krys couldn't see what was inside. We whispered to dad and motioned for him to follow us into the computer room. Dad looked confused watching Kim put on a pair of gloves. She proceed to take the Ziploc bag out of the brown bag very carefully taking one object slowly out at a time and placing them on the computer desk.

"What the hell is this and where did it come from?" He said ferociously.

"It's Krys', need I say more!" Kim blurted out; arms folded. They both look at me. "I'm not speaking this time! Oh God no! I feel like I'm going to throw up." I run to the bathroom in a flash and pull up the seat as I kneel down. My guts were twisting so hard that I felt like last week's food was going to explode out of me. My conscious kicked in as my brain started spinning; I can't confront her on this one. I don't know what to say. I'm not doing it; it will have to be Kim or dad! And that is that!!!

Krystal finally wakes up and heads to the bathroom. I stand by the door to hear her when she is done doing her business before she gets herself high. She finishes and I interrupt her with a knock at the door.

"Are you almost done Krys? I need to go badly, I'm doing the dance out here and it isn't pretty."

"*YES*! Hold on one minute I'm pulling up my pants. Sheesh!" She says with an attitude. The door flings open as I get the evil eye. "Boy someone woke up on the wrong side of the recliner this morning." "Shut up!" She screeches. She goes and sits on the couch as I pretend to go to the bathroom; Kim and dad are already sitting down. I splash my face with water; my face is flushed, butterflies dance through my stomach, I feel nauseas. I think to myself I don't want to do this, I don't want to do this. I slowly walk into the kitchen stalling by making myself a cup of coffee.

I notice the annoyed faces my dad and Kim have as if I'm holding them up because they know I stated I am not talking! Noo *NO*! Krys' face has attitude tattooed all over it. I walk over with my hot coffee and take a seat by Kim. Mo's eyes are swelling trying hard to hold back that tear. I look around the room; I don't like the feeling in the atmosphere. This is all wrong! Should we be going about this like we are? I look at everyone, "*WhaaattT*?" I sip my coffee. I glance at Krystal's legs I watch as I notice them nervously shake up and down so fast and biting her nails. I think to myself she is nervous, she knows something is going on but she can't pinpoint it. Then it happens…. Dad lifts open the couch's arm rest where there is a compartment for keeping your remote and such. He pulls out the Ziploc bag and tosses it to Krystal, then tosses her a glove.

"What is this!?" He spoke firm and steady as a rock.

"It's not mine. It's a friend of mines. He left it in my car the other night when I dropped him off home so his parents wouldn't see it. I forgot to throw it away the other night. I even forgot it was still in my car." Oh she's good! I thought to myself.

Dad snickered at Krystal, "I don't believe you. I may have been born but it wasn't yesterday. Good try though."

Krystal looks around the room, mo bows her face down she can't even look at her in the face, I'm looking at dad in awe, mouth gapping open and Kim is staring Krystal down. Krys is pissed by now, "*WHAT IS THIS!*" She screams. "Some kind of *INTERVENTION*!"

Kim divulges, "Yes as a matter of fact it is and you my dear have a serious problem. You really need to go into rehab." Krystal looks at all of us, tears swell in her eyes and she stomps out of the house.

****

Kyle was the first to find out Krys was hooked on heroine. That's not quite hard when you're a Lt. Detective on the force. He approached us and told us everything. Krys had been taking Josh and leaving for days sometimes weeks. She never answered his calls at all. This was going on for two months, so he was getting suspicious and started snooping around her stuff and found a couple dozen heroine bags and needles hidden. He told us he cannot have this in his house and she needs to move out; he can't take the chance of losing his job. Krystal would have to move in with mom and dad as neither Kim nor I would take her. We couldn't take the chance with our babies at home.

Chapter Nine:
My Sister's Rehab and After

It was barely three months Krys lived with mom and dad and she needed to go to rehab for sure. The septic system was acting up one day and it was frustrating dad. He called someone to come in and find the problem and fix it. Dad was in the house for 5 minutes when the gentleman knocked at the door.

"Come on in." The gentleman walks in and has a perplexed look on his face, "Ah sir. Do you have a diabetic that lives here?"

"No, why would you ask that?"

"Well, why don't you come with me sir."

Dad slips his shoes on and walks outside to the turkey hill where the septic opening is. What he finds as he looks down into the darkened hole were needles; hundreds of them floating on top of the water. He thinks to himself KRYSTAL!!!!!! The gentleman snakes both toilets and pumps out all the needles from the septic system. Later that evening dad had a talk with Krystal and told her she needed to go to rehab. Dad asked Kim and I to find a rehab facility for her.

We got her into Woodland Manor Rehab Facility in Darthwood, PA; three hours away. Their success rate was 99.9%. It seemed like a great place with a very good success rate; maybe we'll get our sister back. She was not happy about going to rehab at all; but we forced her. I think that was our downfall in helping her through her recovery. You see some say that in order for an addict to become clean is that they need to hit rock bottom; and I'll tell you I do believe that to be true. If they don't hit their rock bottom then they don't have the ambition to recover. Also I find that if you push them into getting clean that just adds fuel to the fire.

Mom and dad brought Kristen up to Woodland Manor Rehab Facility on a Monday morning. She had to be there by nine in the morning and since it was a three hour drive they had to leave no later than six am. Knowing my father they left at five thirty. He always had to be early for everything; he was never ever late to anything in his entire life. They stopped down the road from the rehab to kill time. Dad filled the car up with gas and everyone got coffee and a hard roll with butter. They pulled into the parking lot and sat waiting for someone to come out and meet them outside as all doors are locked and only the director has the keys. At five minutes to nine Marissa the director walks out the front door to meet with them.

"Good morning and welcome!" She says with a smile.

"Good morning. Thank you very much." My parents chant in sync. "Ah, this must be Krystal, welcome Krystal. Don't worry you're in good hands." Krys just nods and flashes a quick smile at Marissa. "Well, first I would like to give you all a tour of the place, show you Krystal's room, and Krystal you can meet your roommate. We try to pair the guests up with others whom are most like them to avoid unwanted situations. After the tour we'll go into my office and I'll explain how we do things here and what the rules are. Sound good to you all?" The all nod in unison. "Krystal, are there any nicknames you like to be called?" She mumbles the words softly "Krys." "Ok then. We're off to the tour, come on in Krys, mom and dad."

They enter the building and the tour begins. Krystal meets her roommate Nancy and they hit it off from the start; already Krystal feels at ease. This makes mom and dad very happy and puts them at ease as well. This may be it; her path to recovery. After the tour Marissa leads them to her office where she begins to explain the rules. The first two weeks Krys isn't allowed to have any outside contact with no one; this is the detox stage. After that she will have a schedule of when she can call out to her family and let her family know when they can call her. We were able to attend family fun days unless she hadn't made progress and had taken a step back in her recovery. The program was 30 days long or more depending on how well the person progresses in their recovery. Dad and mom said their final goodbyes and were on their way home; mo cried home the entire three hours.

****

Krystal and her roommate graduated and completed the program in the required thirty days. We were so proud of her. She looked so great; she had color in her face, more meat on her bones and she looked like the sister/daughter we all knew and loved. First thing she did was ask mom and dad to call Kyle and see if it was ok to come by so she may see him and see Josh. The whole time she had been in rehab Kyle took care of Josh for her; he was like a son to Kyle and Josh always accepted him as his one and only dad and still does to this day. Kyle was thrilled to hear she did so well and told them of course she was welcomed to come over.

We had a really nice and enjoyable Welcome home BBQ. It was last minute, but mom and I are great at hosting and doing things last minute; what do you expect we're Italian and the cooks of every holiday! In fact we were partners in crime. The BBQ was a success, mo and I produced a beautiful, delightful spread of food. There was wonderful conversations, laughs, memorable moments brought up and just plain having a blast with our family and children.

Kyle and Krys slipped away, we noticed them walk along Kyle's trails he had throughout his woods. He had beautiful property and very well maintained and taken care of like it was Gold. The trails were lined with circular grey stepping stones. The smell of sweet pine lingers throughout the trails. It was spring time, my most favorite time to walk through his woods.

Not only do I love the smell of the pine but you get to see the trees leaves starting to show a hint of green, Mountain Laurels were starting to bud and open up and you could almost taste their sweet nectar. The blue jays chirped back and forth to each other while the cardinals flew from tree to tree. The beauty of the woods just puts you in a place of serenity and peace.

"Britt, <u>*BRITT*</u>!" Screamed mo. I shook my thoughts away, I must've been daydreaming. "What!" I said annoyed. "Krys has some good news to tell us. She wanted to tell us all at once. Ok, go ahead Krys."

"Well…. Kyle and I had a long talk. We both decided, provided I stay in recovery…."

"*Yes…*" Mo said anxiously with a huge smile on her face. This was the moment she was waiting for.

"I'm moving back and we picked a date for our wedding!" Mom and I screamed happily and ran over and hugged Krys and Kyle. "Wait, you didn't give me the chance to tell you when. It's going to be next June as long as there is a venue open for any Saturday." We congratulated the both of them.

Around July, Krystal stopped by my house with a friend. I had never met this friend, her name was Nancy. I asked Krystal where she met this Nancy and she told me from rehab; they were roommates and graduated with each other. Now I know from Al-Anon that Addicts should never hangout with people they recover if for any reason one should relapse then the other would or may relapse too. When Krys and I had a chance to be alone I told her this. She told me that "I worry too much" she didn't even have an urge to do anything.

Krys and Nancy hung around all the time; it worried me and gave me a horrible gut feeling. I don't know why I did but I know to trust my guts; something was just not right. I shook it off, they seemed fine to me. The girls really like to hang around with me at my house and were there practically every night as I had the weed. So we would smoke a bowl then I would whip up some kind of baked goods for us to snack on; sometimes I'd make several different things depending on how stoned we were, the more we were the more we had the munchies. I was a baker, always loved to bake things like cookies, cakes, pies, pastries, etc.... When my nephew Josh was two and a half years old he always called me "Aunt Britt the great cookie maker."

It was about the week of my middle son and younger daughter's birthday and we were having a combined party for them at Elk Ridge State Park that weekend. Krystal pulls into my driveway as I was smoking a cigarette on the porch. Josh gets out of the car crying and come running to me. A very angered Krystal flings open her back driver side door and looks at me. Inside are Rubbermaid containers stacked up to the top of her car. Krys' anger turned to tears and her tears turned into a waterfall.

I ran to her and pulled her close and held her tight. Rubbing her back I spoke softly "It's ok, I'm here. I'm here… What's going on Krys?"

Mumbling through her tears she says "Kyle and I broke up, he kicked me out. Would you mind if we stay with you until I get a job and can afford a place of our own?"

"Of course you can. I could use the help, been working overtime at mo's office since you went to rehab. She had me take it over; I travel an hour one way to Medford. It winds up being a 12-14 hour day for me. Rich could sure use the help with the kids, cooking and cleaning. What happened? Why did you guys break up?"

Sobbing she replies "I don't want to talk about it, it hurts too much." I didn't say or ask again after that, I respected her feelings and her wishes. I helped her unload her car and then went with her to gather the rest of her things. It was bittersweet.

It was a beautiful day for my children's birthday party. I couldn't have asked for a better day. The sun was shining bright as if she was smiling down upon us, it was hot but not humid; the temperature was Eighty degrees. We were all packed up and on our way to Elk Ridge. We had the pavilion all day long so we started setting up around nine o'clock in the morning.

Elk Ridge had the most beautiful lake with tranquil views. We rented the pavilion for their party; the pavilion had a huge BBQ grill where we could make hot dogs, hamburgers and chicken. The Park had a brand new playground and a beach. The kids could play, swim, fish or go boating. It really was a perfect place to have a birthday party. Krystal and Kim helped me set everything up in the pavilion while the cousins' went and played; except for Hope she had only turned one year old; Mo of course as she did with every baby kept her entertained. I started the grill as it takes awhile for charcoal to heat up and I need to start the chicken first.

Guest start to arrive; they are in awe as they see the delicious spread of food I had made for the party. It really was a perfect day, my friends and family laughed and chatted as they watched all the kids have fun. Richard took the kids fishing all over the lake, down the trails and even half way down the lake. The lake was huge and quite a long walk so he didn't take the children too far from the beach area. Everyone started leaving around six in the evening and some family stayed to help me clean up and pack my car.

I was exhausted when we got home, everyone else unpacked the food and I told them to leave the other stuff not perishable in the car and I would get it later. I laid down on the recliner to relax when Richard came to me and said he had a tick on his belly he had to pull off. I checked to make sure he got the head out as well. There was a red bull's-eye around the infected area. I cleaned it with peroxide as he refused to go to the ER and promised he would go to the doctor as soon as he had time in between clients. That never happened.

A week later I was working at the office when I get a phone call from Krystal saying Richard was taken by ambulance, they think he may have had a stroke. His right side he couldn't feel, his face dropped and he had slurred speech. I talked to the Doctor and said we needed to reschedule the afternoon patients. She told me to go and she would handle it and to let her know if I needed some time off. I rushed to the hospital as fast as I could. I flew into the hospital like a hawk; the lady at the desk directed me to Richards room they had admitted him.

I ran to the elevator and pushed the button to go up, it was taken so long so I kept pushing it and pushing it. It was the longest minute of my life. The people waiting behind me must've thought me to be a lunatic, as I pushed the button again and again until finally I hear that beep and the doors open. My blood was rushing through my veins, heart pumping fast and sweat dripping down my face. I asked the nurse at the nurses' station what room my husband was in, Room 304 she had told me and pointed in the right direction. I got to his room and panic set in; he wasn't there. I thought the worst and ran to the desk asking the nurse where he was. They had taken him down for some tests.

An hour later transport arrived with Richard and I saw his face light up, his right side trying to crack a smile but just stayed drooped. He tried to tell me the tests and what the doctor said but I could not understand completely what he was saying to me. The doctor walked in.

"Hi Richard, how are you doing? You feel any pain, numbness, tingling in your right side?" Richard nods to the doctor but mumbles out no pain. Great this is my time now to ask what is going on with my husband.

"Hi Dr. G. I'm Brittney Owens, Richard's wife. Please explain to me what is going on with him. He was fine all week, completely healthy and showed no signs of having a stroke. Is this possible it could be due to the tick bite, he did have a red bulls-eye around the area from our children's birthday party not this Saturday but last Saturday?"

"Mrs. Owens we are not sure what's going on. We did draw blood and are testing him for Lyme's Disease and we have done some testing for a possible stroke and Bells palsy. He shows symptoms of those two, but not the Lyme's. As soon as I get results I will personally come in and let you know."

I nodded, said my thanks and sat down next to Richard. My anxiety went through the roof waiting to hear from Dr. G for his latest test results; it was killing me inside. I slipped out to have a cigarette as Richard slept and made my phone calls to the immediate family of ours. His mother and Step- father were going to get ready to come up to the hospital. I gave them directions and hoped they wouldn't get lost; they weren't too familiar with Scarlton. I got to room 304 and saw a young gentleman drawing blood; he had to be no older that 25 he must've just graduated. He smiled as he finished and rolled his cart on out of the room. I gave Richard a smile and put his hand in mine and held in lovingly.

"Have to heard anything yet?"

"No. Do that again?"

"Do what again?"

"Rub my hand" I start to rub his hand and massage his fingers. "Britt, I can't feel that. Pinch my left cheek as hard as you can. Then poke my left leg with a pin or something sharp you can find."

"Ok. What's the matter." I become confused and scared at the same time. I pinch his left cheek as hard as I could. He shakes his head in response. I think oh no what the hell now? Then I rummage through my purse and find a safety pin. I start to poke gently up and down his left leg. He shakes his head again.

"Britt I can't feel anything on my left side either. What is going on?" I try not to show my fear as I speed walk out to the desk. I explain what happened and what I did. They immediately page the doctor.

It doesn't take long for Dr G. to come to Richard's room; this time he came with another doctor. "Mr. and Mrs. Owens all the test results were normal, he didn't have a stroke and doesn't have Bells palsy. This is Dr Schoonover he is a neurologist and is going to examine you Richard and do some more testing. The examination took about ten minutes; which I felt wasn't sufficient enough. He ordered a CT scan with and without contrast of his brain. I am hoping he will find some answers."

After all tests have been done both Doctor's asked Rich's mom and I to come with them into a private room to discuss his health and results of the tests. The doctors were baffled as to why Rich was paralyzed from the waist down, he had been in the hospital for about seven days now and had regained function in his arms and face once again, but from the waist down he was still paralyzed. All test results came out normal; they told us the only conclusion they could come up with was that he had ALS. That diagnosis wasn't good enough for my mother-in-law and I. We insisted on them giving him a spinal tap that something else was going on and they weren't looking deep enough. The doctors felt like we were insulting their knowledge of medicine. I didn't care, something did this to my husband

and I wasn't going down without a fight. They told us there was no need to put him through a spinal tap.

The eighth day Richard came home. The hospital let us go without any wheelchair; how ridiculous of them knowing he couldn't walk. I had to find help to buy a wheelchair for him. Thank goodness for our community; they raised money to buy him a new wheelchair. Krys was now on her own taking care of four children, with Rich being paralyzed and limited to help her and myself working ten hours with a two hour commute round trip; she quickly became stressed out.

I noticed a change in Krystal towards the end of July of 2011despite the fact that Rich had picked up on it sooner and had warned me. I didn't believe him. My husband and younger sister never had a really good relationship; it was a love hate relationship. So I thought it was just his nonsense trying to get rid of her as they fought all the time. Krys had become attitudinal, slacking on keeping the house clean and sleeping a lot; leaving Rich to take care of the children. When both adults slept my oldest son, Kevin whom was ten at the time was forced to care for the younger children. It made me think of my childhood and having to grow up fast; this is not what I wanted for any of my children.

Krystal began sleeping during the day and up all night, her face had become sunken and black bags under her eyes. I started to become suspicious of her relapsing. My guts were twisting all the time and I dreaded going to work every morning worrying about my children and nephew. I'd get phone calls from Keith almost every day crying to me about how Aunt Krystal and dad were sleeping and neither would wake up. He had to make lunch for the kids and watch them; my poor child didn't have a good summer and I felt at fault for it.

It had gotten worse with Krystal when she kept bringing strange people around my house. I've never seen them around town before in my life. They would only come around at night. I wanted to spit and throw up all at once. I knew something was up and that something was not good.

****

Mid September 2011

Things took a turn for the worse with Richard; he started having chest pains and sharp pains down his left arm. I called my parents and his mom and told them what was going on and that I was making the hour commute to Elmira Medical Center (EMC) in Elmira, PA. Elmira is where his mom lives and where Rich and I met when we both attended Elmira University. I told them I was not going back to Scarlton General Hospital (SGH), I did not trust their doctor's. We arrived at EMC in forty minutes, record time; I was driving so fast trying to get him their incase he was having a heart attack. His mother was already at the emergency room entrance waiting for us. She had a wheelchair ready for Rich. I dropped him off to his mother to get him registered and went to park the car; parking is horrendous there, you can never find a spot.

The ER was packed with a lot of people; some with the flu, some there just to get their usual fix of pain meds and some with the bug. They took Rich right in as he was a possible heart attack patient and that's top priority. We were put into a rather large and long room. The nurse who took his vitals and wheeled him in helped him to transfer from the wheelchair to the bed. She spoke softly and concerned asking Rich about his symptoms and what happened that he had become paralyzed. We explained the story as she took notes.

She said "I will talk to the doctor on call about all of this and I'll order an EKG and stress test for the time being and see what that brings. The doctor on call is Dr. Bahaullah, everyone just loves him he is a very great and kind doctor. Don't worry you're in good hands." We all smiled and gave her a pleasant nod.

Before we knew it they were taking Rich up for his tests. I looked at my mother-in-law, eyes popping out and a gapping mouth. "Wow that was quick."

"I know, odd this hospital really isn't this efficient and quick. Maybe it's because he is so young they've taken a sense of urgency." We both shrugged our shoulders and just started chatting to pass the time. Ten minutes go by as a very tall, young gentleman walks in; he looks to be in his late forties.. He has perfect short black hair, beautiful big brown eyes, he walked in with confident flashing us a warm welcoming smile, showing those pearly white teeth. He was wearing a lab coat and scrubs, his badge said Dr. Behad Bahaullah, neurologist. He introduced himself to the both of us and shook our hand firmly. He asked us what happened as we told him the nightmare we went through at SGH. He listens to us very concerned about how they treated Rich and gave him a diagnosis that they didn't even do the correct test for.

"You can't even diagnose ALS without doing a spinal tap. Have they performed one on him?"

Annoyed at the doctors from SGH I spoke "No they didn't Dr. Bahaullah; they felt it wasn't necessary and didn't think they need to put him through that. They just diagnosed him with the ALS and said his paralyzation should get better in time. They sent us on our way without a wheel chair knowing fully well Richard couldn't walk." My voice was angered at this point. "I'm sorry Dr. Bahaullah for raising my voice it was so frustrating and if you only knew…"

He cut me off, "No need for apologies Mrs. Owens. He was angered and appalled hearing our story. In a loud voice he shouted "Nurse Kathy, can you please come here. Order Richard's family whatever they would like to eat and drink on me. Then I would like you to schedule me a spinal tap on Mr. Owens as soon as his other tests are finished, I want him to go right from the last test to the OR I will be ready and waiting. I also would like you to let the lab know I want those results rushed immediately, give them a heads up so they are prepared. Don't worry Mrs. Owens and mom he is in good hands." I felt a sigh of relief and felt finally some doctor who really cares and is willing to find out what was going on with my husband.

About an hour later in came transport with Rich's face down on a hospital bed; the head part was cut out so his face fit inside to breathe. In walks Dr. B he has a sullen look on his face. "The good news is he does not have ALS. I had thought he may have had Gillian Barre syndrome, but he doesn't." He takes a deep breath. My heart races and I squeeze Rich's hand tight. "We found spirochetes in his spinal fluid. He has Stage three spinal neuro Lyme's disease. This is why it has affected Rich so quickly, made it seem like he had a stroke, bells palsy and paralyzed him. The spirochetes masks' the Lyme's and makes it seem like the patient is suffering from something else with no explanation. I would like to admit him to the hospital under my care and give him a heavy dose of antibiotics and start him on the healing process. I am hoping it is not too late."

I was relieved, finally a doctor willing to help us and one who believed us. I hugged Dr. B with tears in my eyes. "Thank you so much Dr. Bahaullah, you don't know what this means to us." He smiled and walked out of the room. I could hear him at the nurses' station telling them to get Rich a room ASAP, he wanted to start treatment right away.

****

Richard had been in the hospital for 3 weeks now, my life was in turmoil. I was working a lot, trying to double book during the morning and early afternoon so I could go to the hospital to visit Rich then be home for my children for dinner and bedtime. I had to rely on Krystal who was a hot mess and my guts twisted every day I left my children entrusted in her care. I had to be strong; I had to show no weakness, I couldn't fall apart. No my children needed me; they need to see that everything was going to be ok with their dad. The walls were crumbling, I was dying inside. I couldn't show that to any one I had to hold my head up high and show everybody that I was tough and I could get through anything life threw at me. My anxiety grew and my smoking increased. I smoked on the way to work and on the way home. It was the pot that kept me going, it kept me strong and gave me the will to keep going on and stay positive. That's all I could do was to stay positive. At home things got worse; I got phone calls every day from Keith about Aunt Krys. Either she was sleeping or nowhere to be found. Panic set in, I knew.... I had this gut feeling she had relapsed.

After three weeks of Richard being on the treatment Dr. B had him on he had an adverse reaction to it and ended up in ICU. They had to put a breathing tube in him; he couldn't breathe on his own. Dr. B had to slowly bring him down off the treatment and start him on something new. He had been in the hospital for a month and a half when the insurance cut him off and said no more treatments and he had to be discharged.

Dr. B was heartbroken; he believed this treatment was working. His tests showed some improvements in his legs; his right toes wiggled and he had hope. Despite the fact the treatment was working and Dr. B fought with the insurance for us they refused to pay anymore and insisted he be discharged that day.

Back on the home front tension grew between Richard and Krystal; I was barely home back to working my twelve hour days. Rich would call me and tell me how Krys would just leave for hours. He would scoot up the stairs and search her room as he has suspicions of her relapse. He knew she was using. I wasn't home enough to pick up on the clues. I didn't believe him; this caused a lot of friction and fighting between us as I had no proof of her using. Until one evening…..

It was three in the morning and I was awoken suddenly my front door slammed shut and I heard loud talking and laughing. I grabbed my robe and opened my bedroom door peeking around the corner to look down the stairs. I see a strange black man standing by my door. He looks like he is doped out, not just on marijuana, but something else. I walk down furious and start to yell "<u>Who the hell</u> are you and what the hell are you doing in my house?"

"Sorry for waking you, I'm a friend of Krystal's."

My guts twisted as I spoke frantically to this stranger "Where is she?"

"She went to the bathroom."

I ran hysterically to the bathroom and flung the door open to a startled Krystal about to inject some sort of liquid in her arm. I was enraged with fire in my eyes. She knew she was caught and would have to face the devil, me. I made her inject the liquid in the toilet and flush it. I told her to put the cap on the needle and give it to me. I went to the kitchen grabbed an empty can of soda, snapped the needle off and put it and the syringe into the can and crushed it. I looked at Krys and told her to get her druggy friend out of my house or I will grab him by his collar and personally throw him out through my door to ensure he won't ever come back here again. I told her if he came around again I will personally remove him from my property and call the cops on him.

I woke up early the next morning and called my parents. I spoke to my father and told him about last night and how she can no longer stay in my house anymore. But I didn't have the heart to kick her out, I needed backup. Kim was up visiting for the weekend so she came over with dad. We sat at the table and discussed what we were going to do and how we were going to discuss things with Krystal. We decided that she needed to give Guardianship of Josh over to me; she had no choice or say in the matter. We already had the papers filled out and just needed to sign in front of the notary and lawyer.

Krystal came downstairs all sleepy eyed, yawning as she stretched her arms out and behind her neck. Her mouth gapped open as she saw the three of us at the kitchen table.

"What is this? Another freaking intervention?" She said as she rolled her eyes.

I was appalled; she didn't realize the extent or damage she could have done to anyone of these children. "Krys do you not realize that you not only put yourself in danger, but our children as well. Hope is starting to walk around; what if she were to get one of your needles that would kill her!" A tear rolls down her face, she is silent. "I'm sorry but I can't take that chance with my children or your child." I cry, it was the hardest thing I have ever done. Will she ever forgive me?

"I pray for the enlightenment to make my detachment loving, not cruel. Let it not be a wall between us, but a bond of mutual respect for one another's individuality.")*

Dad clears his voice; it is stern as he speaks to her "You are going to stay with Kim. You <u>WILL</u> do as she says. You will not be left alone. She will take you to NA three times a week or more, however many times she thinks you need. You will also sign over Guardianship of Josh to Britt for three years. That should give you plenty of time to get sober, if not then you will sign for another three years and so on. Is all this understood?" She looks at each one of us, tears cascade down her face. She nods unenthusiastically.

****

November 2011

Krystal stayed sober for two and a half months when she stayed with Kim. Everything was going well "according to Kim," we had many arguments on the phone as I didn't believe Krys was doing well. My guts told me differently, just by some of the things Kim told me how she acted. I told Kim not to let her guard down. If there was one thing I learned from my experience with living in turmoil with a drug addict it was to trust my gut instinct!

It wasn't until 2 weeks before Christmas that Kim finally believed me as she cleaned Krystal's room one day. I received a disturbing call from her, she was crying. She apologized to me and told me I was right. As she cleaned Krys' room she found several burn marks on the bed and carpet, which were hidden by furniture and clothing. After the holidays Kim had to kick Krystal out, she too had two little kids and couldn't take the chance of them getting hurt by Krys' addiction. We heard Krystal moved to Philadelphia with this guy named Fred who was her boyfriend. We tried to keep in touch but she never returned phone calls or never visited. She never called her son and barely showed for family functions. It was like she just vanished.

I never said it but in my head I said "I told you so." Kim and I tried to help our little sister. She didn't want help from rehab, from me and now from Kim. You can't help an addict unless they want to be helped, or unless they hit "Rock bottom" as they call it. I thought me taking Josh from her would be her hitting her "Rock bottom," but now I realize it just gave her the freedom she needed. Sometimes when I thought about it back then I blamed myself, I enabled her to continue. I gave her that freedom to be able to do what she pleased.

*"Progress begins when we stop trying to control the uncontrollable and when we go on to correct what we have the right to change. If we accept a situation full of misery and uncertainty, it is no one's fault but our own. We can do something about it! Either do something or quit fretting.")**

Chapter Ten:
Change, Strength, Courage and Hope

Everyone has a chance to make their own path in life. It's that choice, that path you make that shapes who you are today. You can choose that long, beaten, rocky path with a dark tunnel at the end or you can choose the long, straight, with few bumps (life lessons') with a light at the end. Only <u>YOU</u> can decide….

2014

Everything was going great in the household, the kids were flourishing, even Josh. I had him in therapy since his mother left to go live with Aunt Kim. He was doing so well, but some anger built up inside. He talked to me often, I felt honored he was comfortable in telling me such things, such emotions.

The kids were in school when I received a phone call. It was Krystal. I hadn't spoken to her in over a year. I was shocked.

"Wow, Hi Krys. How are you? I haven't heard from you in a long time, too long." I hear a muffled sniffle. "You ok Krys?"

I hear her take a deep breath, "Britt I'm sober. I have been these past three years. I wanted to ask you if you would please give me a second chance and let me stay with you until I get back on my feet." I could hear her breathing heavy, her chest heaving waiting for me to say that dreaded word.... No.

"Krys, how am I supposed to believe a word you say? You lied to me the whole time you were living with me. It was one lie after another, after another. And I believed you, like a fool I believed you! You were using and that was forbidden in my house. Not only did you lie to me but you lied to yourself. You created such turmoil in my home and put not only my children but your child in danger as well. I haven't even heard from you in over a year. I call you or text you and I get no response. You know what that seems like to me, you are still using in my eyes. When you hide from the people who love you the most like you've done in the past it's a sign of drug use. So you tell me how can I believe you this time?"

The phone is silent, followed by a soft whimper. I can picture her face, tears streaming down her cheeks as she wipes them away to regain control in her voice. Her voice cracks as she clears it "Britt things are different now. I want to tell you something I've never told anyone. You remember meeting Fred a couple of times; he isn't the person he portrayed himself to be to all of you. He has been beating me for four years now. I have been in and out of the hospital, I've had two miscarriages. I can't even count anymore how many bones he has broken."

I am appalled, I don't know what to believe, could this be one of her lies? I have doubts. "He has threatened me that if I ever touch cocaine, heroin or any other illicit drug other than marijuana he would kill me. In a way he has made me sober, but I am scared. I'm trapped; he keeps me locked up in his house all day long until he comes home from work. I'm not allowed anywhere without him and if I ever talk to a guy boy do I get the beating of my life when we get home. I can't take anymore, I need help. Britt I don't care bring down a test and test me. *PLEASE*! You will find nothing in my system but THC. I need you; I need the support of my family. I need my son…" I hear her sobbing and it breaks my heart.

"Ok, I will bring a test down and I swear if you're not clean you stay. I will show you no sympathy, no remorse. You will get a job and help around the house and if you <u>EVER</u> lie to me again, you're done; I don't want to know you anymore. Understood?"

I hear a sigh of relief in her voice "Thank you. We have to do this when he is at work, he cannot know or he will surely kill me. He works tomorrow ten in the morning until seven at night. Best time to come would be between eleven and two. I will have my things packed."

"Ok, Kim and I will be there at eleven to help you pack so we can get you out of their faster. Is she allowed to know?"

"You can tell her, I can't. I just want this part of my life over and start my life anew. I waited three years as promised, though it was hell. In a way I am grateful to Fred. He got me sober, but in a way I resent him. What and how he kept me sober was wrong but it worked."

One question circled around in my head; I just had to ask to ensure the safety of my family. "How do you know that he won't come to my house for you? After all he does know where I live."

"Britt, he is afraid of you. I told him the story of how you beat up a four hundred thirty-five pound man right in front of our family's eyes. I told him if he didn't believe me to ask dad, he doesn't lie and he was as shocked as the rest of us. He tried to stop you and you had the strength to knock him off you and he went down to the ground. He will not come anywhere near you. Believe me, your house is the safest place for me."

I agreed. We said our goodbyes and hung up the phone. I immediately called Kim after I got off the phone. I explained the whole situation with Krystal, she told me that Krys called her some months back and asked her if she would pick her up from the hospital. She was beaten so bad her face was unrecognizable. Kim allowed her to stay at her house for a week and Krys went back after Fred begged her to. Like a fool she fell prey to his lies. It was a vicious cycle for her; I couldn't even imagine what she went through.

The following day Kim and I met at Krystal's apartment to pick her up. I was nervous; nervous because I didn't know what to expect. I had never been to this part of Philly; I've heard South side was a bad part. We went down the alley way to her apartment; it should have been a one way. There were cars parked on both sides of the alley and not enough room for two cars to drive through. The apartments were in rows on both sides of the road. They were red brick, some looked nice and some looked disgusting. Every house had a dark curtain in their front window; hmm I wonder why?

We arrived at Krystal's apartment, her apartment was the only one without a dark curtain and the window contain some remnants' of Christmas decorations left over from the holidays. There was no room for me to park my car so I was forced to go to the end of the alley and make a right at the corner. As I wait for traffic to clear I notice several people on the corner passing something back and forth carefully. I try not to look as not to bring any attention to us. I whisper to Kim without turning my head and ask her if her door was locked. I was relieved to know all doors were locked and windows were closed. My heart was pumping waiting for the traffic to break as I notice an older black gentleman approach my car. Panic starts to set in. *Oh lord please traffic, please let up.* I hear a knock at my window and I freeze. Both Kim and I look at the gentleman as he opens his trench coat to reveal some burned DVD's and some drugs. He looks at us and points to each thing giving us thumbs up then pointing to the corner across the street. I shook my head frantically and peeled out not knowing there was a car quickly approaching the right lane, cutting the car off. I circle around the block back towards Krys' ally noticing a car leaving I hit the gas speeding to take the parking spot. I look at Kim her face pale, chest heaving, her knuckles white from holding onto the handle so tight; I apologize for scaring the shit out of her. I grab my purse and take out my pocket knife holding it in the palm of my hand for protection; keeping it hidden.

We walked twelve apartments down to get to Krystal's. We knock desperately, no answer. Now I am scared as I notice out the corner of my eye that same gentleman walking towards us. Hysterically I knock louder and louder not stopping until the door is answered. Kim and I rush into the door and I slam it shut locking the door behind and let out a deep breath. We are greeted by a young girl with curly, brown hair and brown eyes. She looks to be about eleven years old. She greets us with a warm smile and introduces herself.

The apartment was permeated by the smell of cigarettes and marijuana. The first room was the living room, the carpet and coach had tears and were filthy; not the way I would like to live. The Christmas tree was still up and there was a huge Barbie house set up besides the tree. It was a mess with furniture and Barbie dolls all over the place. To the left was the kitchen, in my opinion I would never cook in it. There were parts of linoleum missing from the floor, counter tops full of dirty dishes, spilt cereal or some kind of food and drinks. The sink was old and loaded to the top with nasty, molded dishes. I was repulsed by the sight of it all. I looked at Kim; she too looked squeamish at the sight. I decide not to go see the bathroom for fear bugs would come rushing out as I turn the light on.

Krystal runs down the stairs with several black garbage bags. She looked really good; she had gained weight and her face gained color. The black bags under her eyes were no longer there. I could tell she hadn't done anything. For the first time I had real Hope for my baby sis.

"What the hell took you so long?!! Do you know what we went through? Some guy was following us trying to sell us drugs and stuff." I let it all out in one breath. My voice and body shaky as my anxiety is labored. I put my knife in my pocket for when we leave this hell hole.

"Oh my, I am so sorry Britt. I have everything packed, let's go. Sarah please let your dad know I went food shopping with my sisters." The young child nods her head as she hugs Krystal and cries.

We were finally home. I helped Krys bring her stuff inside. Josh came running downstairs and runs to his mom and hugged her so tight. Tears flowed from my eyes as well as mom and sons. I help Krys settle in and gave her, her own room back. We kept all medicines locked up in the safe so she had no weakness to relapse. After all she had not touched pills, cocaine or heroin in three years.

Krys was exuberant, her attitude was different, she was her happy joking self; she was my little sister again. She kept her promise on keeping up with the house and taking care of Rich and the children. It was about four months when she came to me and asked to speak to me in private. She told me she was four months late and that we needed to get a pregnancy test. We went immediately to the store and bought one; she was pregnant. She asked me to keep this a secret; she wanted to think how she was going to tell mom and dad about this. I did as asked; in my mind I was elated this baby could keep her on the right path in her recovery especially if the baby is a girl.

Krystal was starting to show her baby bump and had to break the news to mom and dad. I brought her over to their house and stood by her side as her support system. She told them everything from the past, her recovery and now being pregnant with Fred's baby. Mom was thrilled as usual, dad didn't say a word. He got up from his recliner, walked up the stairs to his computer room. Mom told Krys not to worry about him, he would get over it. Krys decided she couldn't leave things like this and went upstairs to talk to him.

Mom and I went to Krys' first sonogram; she was six months pregnant and we were hoping that we'd be able to find out the sex of the baby. The technician told us everything was great with the baby and if we wanted to know what Krys was having. The three of us shouted YES in unison. The technicians smiled; she told us it was a girl. Krys cried she was finally having her girl! Inside I had a party going on, I knew what this meant. Her path to recovery was going to be hopeful. She now has a reason besides Josh.

Faith Drea was born June 6th 2015. I loved the name Krys picked out for Faith Drea; it means Hope and Courage. I was convinced now more than ever that Krystal was on the right path. I enjoyed the time that the three of them lived with me and the day came when Krys was ready to fly all by herself. I cried, I couldn't help but to be proud of her and proud of myself for playing a role in helping her finding her way to the light….. I am proud to say that Krystal has not gone back to pills, cocaine or heroin in six years.

****

2016

I take a deep breath…. "Hi, my name is Brittney and I am an addict. My drug of choice is marijuana." I don't know why but I proceed to tell my story, I don't tell all of it just recent incidents and all the turmoil of what my life is now. Somehow I feel comfort in this group; the people seem concerned and sympathetic as I tell my story of how I came to be here at DATS, how I started to dance with the devil…

Everyone has a story to tell; whether it be bad or worse than the next person. But in my experience from my families' addictions I have learned that you cannot help the addict who doesn't want help. You can't force them into getting help; you can however just be there to let them know you are there for them when they need you. Let them know that you love them; show them that you won't give up on them. You have to find the hope, strength and courage in yourself to go on. You need to be accepting of the fact that addiction is an illness before you can help the unwilling.

Addiction is a disease, a compulsion and like any other disease it needs to be treated. But treatment of this disease is long term, it's a constant struggle. Even the addict that has been sober for twenty-five or thirty years still struggles and still have those moments of cravings. It's their will, their strength, courage and hope that keeps them from relapse.

These are the memoirs of an alcohol, drug addicted family……

"I pray for the realization that the addict is sick and desperate, and I ask that I be given the strength to help him/her in the right and constructive way."

Chapter Eleven:

Serenity Prayer: Keep It Simple

<u>Serenity prayer</u>*

God. Grant me the SERENITY to change the things I cannot,

COURAGE to change the things I can,

And the WISDOM to know the difference!

*ONE DAY AT A TIME**

Chapter Twelve:
The Twelve Steps and Traditions

The Twelve Steps

1. We admit we were powerless over alcohol that our lives have become unmanageable.

2. Came to believe that a Power greater than ourselves could restore us to sanity.

3. Made a decision to turn our will and lives over to the care of God as we understood Him.

4. Made a searching and fearless moral inventory of ourselves.

5. Admitted to God, to ourselves, and to another human being the exact nature of our wrongs.

6. Were entirely ready to have God remove all these defects of character.

7. Humbly ask Him to remove our shortcomings.

8. Made a list of all persons we have harmed, and became willing to make amends to them all.

9. Made direct amends to such people wherever possible, except when to do so would injure them or others.

10. Continued to take personal inventory and when we were wrong promptly admitted it.

11. Sought through prayer and meditation to improve our conscious contact with God as we understood Him, praying only for knowledge of His will for us and the power to carry that out.

12. Having has a spiritual awakening as a result of these steps, we tried to carry this message to others, and to practice these principles in all our affairs.

The Twelve Traditions

1. Our common welfare should come first; personal progress for the greatest number depends upon unity.

2. For our group there is but one authority a loving God as He may express Himself in our group conscious. Our leaders are but trusted servants they do not govern.

3. The relatives of alcoholics, when gathered together for mutual aid, may call themselves an Al-Anon family group, provided that, as a group, they have no other affiliation. The only requirement for membership is that there be a problem of alcoholism in a relative or friend.

4. Each group should be anonymous, except in matters affecting another group or Al-Anon or AA as a whole.

5. Each Al-Anon Family group has but one purpose: to help families of alcoholics. We do this by practicing the Twelve Steps of AA

ourselves, by encouraging and understanding our alcoholic relatives, and by welcoming and giving comfort to families of alcoholics.

6. Our Family Groups ought never endorse, finance or lend our name to any outside enterprise, lest problems of money, property and prestige divert us from our primary spiritual aim. Although a separate entity, we should always co-operate with Alcoholics Anonymous.

7. Every group ought to be fully self-supporting, declining outside contributions.

8. Al-Anon Twelfth Step work should remain forever non-professional, but our service centers may employee special workers.

9. Our groups, as such, ought never be organized; but we may create service boards or committees directly responsible to those they serve.

10. The Al-Anon Family Groups have no opinion on outside issues; hence our name ought never be drawn into public controversy.

11. Our public relations policy is based on attraction rather than promotion; we need always maintain personal anonymity at the level of press, radio, films and TV. We need guard with special care the anonymity of all AA members.

12. Anonymity is the spiritual foundation of all our Traditions, ever reminding us to place principles above personalities.

These Traditions are your guidelines to help your personal growth and keep your life growing. Now I'm not saying that you have to practice these everyday of your life; I say at least once do each step one by one finishing the first then moving to the next until you're all finished. When you feel like your life has become unmanageable and you feel powerless, go ahead. Go to a meeting, It'll do you some good. "Let Go, Let God")*

Epilogue

♦ ♦ ♦

2016

I am divorced almost a year now; separated for two years. I live with my boyfriend and my ex has put us through hell. He has lied and called CYS constantly saying I abuse my three children taking my children away from me. My life spiraled out of control when my mom passed away just about one year ago from Metastatic Breast Cancer of the Liver, Bones and Ménages of the Brain. He used my breakdown against me at my weakest moment of my life.

The day of her funeral I wasn't myself, I wasn't coherent. Who in their right mind would leave me with six children to care for? I wasn't right in the head, I wasn't there; I was empty.... The hour long ride home from Stanton to Jackson was a blur to me. I was numb, I never heard the kids fighting or calling my name; my face was pale and blank. We arrived at my sister's place with the kids. My boyfriend dropped us off and quick runs home and changes then comes back to help me with the kids until both my sisters come back. I wasn't aware of what was going to happen next, I blacked out. When I came to my son Keith was holding me in the road, I was lying in front of a car and the driver was calling my name. I heard muffled voices; Keith was crying "mom are you ok?" I blacked out again and began shaking, I couldn't catch my breath. I felt my body being moved, muffled voices of kids crying, calling my name, asking me if I was ok; people screaming call 911. A complete stranger gathered the children to bring them inside the house, Keith refused to leave me. I was coming to my eyes opening to see Keith and all these strangers surrounding me. I panicked and started hyperventilating. I couldn't breathe; Keith got scared and held me tight rocking me back and forth in his arms whispering "Calm down mom it's ok breath in and out slowly. You can do it. Everyone please back away she needs space, she just lost her mom and is having a panic attack, please give her room to breathe."

I black out again as Keith cries and screams "no mom stay with me please." "I'm here Keith, I'm here, and mommy isn't going anywhere." But he doesn't hear me, no one does. No words escape my mouth. I hear muffled voices, my eyes open slightly to see two EMT's working on me, one puts a blood pressure cuff on me and the other an oxygen mask. I black out again and hear the gentleman say hurry she is tachycardic we need to go now. My body starts twitching and trembling as my hyperventilating begins again. "Help me I can't breathe I scream." But no one hears me. I black out again.

I awaken in the ambulance to the sound of the wailing and everyone poking and prodding at me. I start to freak out. "Where are my children!! My nieces and nephews???" A gentle voice says "Don't worry Ms. Owens they are fine your sisters came home and your boyfriend will meet us in the ER. What happened?" They told me what had happened according to my son and witnesses. I start hyperventilating knowing that my son had to deal with this and the children saw what happened. I started freaking out trying to pull my IV out, "I need to go back to them, they need me."

"Ms. Owens, you need to take care of yourself first. You just ran in front of a car and tried to kill yourself."

I broke down and started freaking out. Noooo I screamed out in my head. I started to wiggle and writhed as they injected a clear liquid into my IV. I started to calm into a deep sleep. Next thing I knew I was being wheeled into the hospital, lights fading in and out, I see my boyfriend concern on his face as he grabs my hand. "Mel, are you ok? I love you, please don't do that again." I try to mumble words out but nothing. I fade out only hearing soft mumbling and not understanding what anyone is saying. Nurses come into my room hooking liquids up to my IV, taking blood and hooking wires up to my chest. My boyfriend talking with the doctor's and the crisis worker. I am in a deep sleep, all I see is darkness. I am dancing in the dark….

References

♦ ♦ ♦

1. *The book of Al-Anon & Alcoholics Anonymous*
2. *The book of Al-Ateen: Hope for Children of Alcoholics*
3. *One Day at a Time in Al-Anon*
4. *Thomas Merton: No Man is an Island*

www.ingramcontent.com/pod-product-compliance
Lightning Source LLC
Chambersburg PA
CBHW021447070526
44577CB00002B/290